THE DOCTOR

Once a Cluefinder,
Always a Cluefinder!

keep on Shining like the
gem you are ♥

THE DOCTOR

The Toxic Combination of Love,
Hatred, and Revenge Is Served

Sally Barrilla

NEW DEGREE PRESS

THE DOCTOR
The Toxic Combination of Love, Hatred, and Revenge Is Served

ISBN
978-1-63730-828-8   *Paperback*
978-1-63730-890-5   *Kindle Ebook*
978-1-63730-960-5   *Digital Ebook*

CONTENTS

——

CHAPTER   NOTE FROM THE AUTHOR   11

PART 1   **PART 1**   **15**

CHAPTER 1   THE NIGHTMARE BEGINS   17

CHAPTER 2   A DAY IN THE LIFE OF SASHA   21

CHAPTER 3   WE NEED TO STICK TOGETHER   25

CHAPTER 4   THE CALL   31

CHAPTER 5   THE INEVITABLE ARRIVES   35

CHAPTER 6   LEARNING THE TRUTH   39

PART 2   **PART 2**   **45**

CHAPTER 7   MEANING OF LIFE   47

CHAPTER 8   ANIMOSITY HAS NO PLACE
FOR COMPANIONSHIP   51

CHAPTER 9   THE PLAN IS IN ACTION   55

CHAPTER 10   TAKING A STEP CLOSER TO HER   59

CHAPTER 11   HITTING THE BREAKING POINT   63

CHAPTER 12   KILLERS DON'T REFORM   67

CHAPTER 13   JUMPING INTO THE WELL
OF DR. JONATHAN MORGAN   71

CHAPTER 14   BLISS DOESN'T LAST LONG   75

CHAPTER 15   DREAMCATCHER OF GOODWILL   79

CHAPTER 16   HOW LOW CAN YOU GO?   83

CHAPTER 17   A BREAK IN THE CURTAIN   87

PART 3.   **PART 3**   **91**

CHAPTER 18   THE KISS OF DEATH   93

CHAPTER 19   AN UNLIKELY ACQUAINTANCE   97

CHAPTER 20   SHIT HITS THE FAN, LIFE GIVES
YOU LEMONS, MAKE A FRIEND   101

CHAPTER 21   I GOTTA GO MY OWN WAY   107

CHAPTER 22   CONSPIRING WITH A SIDEKICK   113

CHAPTER 23   THE SHOW MUST GO ON   117

PART 4.   **PART 4**   **121**

CHAPTER 24   LIVING A LIE   123

CHAPTER 25   THE LADY AND THE TRAMP   125

CHAPTER 26   ADD FUEL TO THE FIRE   129

CHAPTER 27   EXPLORING A NEW HUMAN   133

CHAPTER 28   JUST BEING ALIVE   137

CHAPTER 29   FORGETTING THE PLAN   141

PART 5.   **PART 5**   **147**

CHAPTER 30   THE ROMANTIC OBSTACLE   149

CHAPTER 31   A RECONFIGURATION OF THE HEART   155

CHAPTER 32   SASHA FINALLY SUCCEEDS   161

CHAPTER 33   THE FINALE: WHEN HEAVEN
FINALLY MEETS HELL PART 1   165

CHAPTER 34   THE FINALE: WHEN HEAVEN
FINALLY MEETS HELL PART 2   169

CHAPTER 35   THE FINALE: WHEN HEAVEN
FINALLY MEETS HELL PART 3   175

CHAPTER 36   THE TRIAL RESOLUTION OF SASHA   183

ACKNOWLEDGMENTS   189

"Mama, why is my doctor hurting me? The pain doesn't stop. I can't do this. What's happening to me? I can't feel my legs or my face. Am I going to die?"

JACKSON THOMAS, HIS LAST WORDS TO HIS MOTHER, PRIVATE DETECTIVE SASHA THOMAS

NOTE FROM
THE AUTHOR

———

Dear Reader,

Roses are red, violets are blue, looking for the next chill down your bones? Then this book is for you!

This psychological thriller is fictional, but its intensifying story will cause goosebumps to creep up all over your skin with a surprising twist upon the finale.

But in all seriousness, this book is for anyone who ever wanted to take a walk down the dark, wild side. I wrote it coming from my personal experiences of being bullied in school, by family members, and by several relatives. I wondered about being someone different from who I was, someone who knew how to fight back against attackers, striving for justice, and, most importantly, someone who does not allow anxiety and depression to stop her from achieving what she wishes.

I was always so curious to explore our inner darkness, the "devilish" part of us that many of us suppress, to push past our inner selves and gain a new type of confidence! For example, let's say you are driving somewhere, and someone cuts right in front of you or tailgates you, and you choose to let it go and not to fight back. What would we become if we could embody the opposite of our normal selves? How do we explore our inner darkness to get revenge, to fight back?

The antihero and protagonist, Sasha, is on a mission of revenge against a doctor of death who, instead of healing his patients, murders them. Sasha's son, Jackson, becomes one of his many victims. However, little does Sasha know her desire to destroy Dr. Morgan will ultimately either make or break her entire life.

I first came up with my alter ego, Sasha, when I was in fifth or sixth grade. After a particularly traumatic incident with those considered "the cool girls" at school, I thought of a young woman who looked exactly like me but was nothing like me.

What was she like? What did she do in her spare time? Who were her friends? Who did she trust? Did she confide in others too easily as I did? Did she enjoy writing as I do? How did she manage through life? Did she also have anxiety and suffer from depression? I wanted to know more about my "identical twin." I mean, if she was in my mind rent-free twenty-four seven, why not get to know just who she was?

This book will take the reader along with me on this story I've crafted to see all these aspects. If someone hurts the ones we love, how far can we go to avenge them, to get revenge? How far can trauma and loss push us?

I felt compelled to write because I'd like to help you explore your inner darkness. How do we explore our inner darkness? Who truly knows what is right versus wrong? Does it depend on the circumstance or the person's upbringing?

As stated previously, I wanted to create a character who is the opposite of me—outspoken, a total badass, trying to get revenge against someone who took away what she loved the most. Her dream ripped out of her hands.

As a former English honors major with a creative writing specialization, I recall reading many of Stephen King's books in college. I remember feeling fascinated with the concept of utilizing your experiences and turning them into brilliant stories.

Quoting a former professor who emphasized that "Your history matters, it doesn't matter whether or not you are famous. Your history is important and makes up a part of the past, present, and future."

Essentially, I also then realized if you can't find the words, write them down.

This book symbolizes how, even in trying or troubling times, one can use this as fuel to create beautiful things. Or perhaps something about how compelling and beautiful artistry can spring forth from darkness and ugliness—showing deeper emotion than ever known before.

Furthermore, I would like to help my readers learn from my antihero, for anyone who considers themselves as soft-spoken to explore living in their own fantasy, to live out that wish, and give you an antihero to look up to. An inner self-reflection (doppelgänger). I made her the antihero because she's not perfect, but she's not evil. It's just the lesson that shows that life made her that way. Life grants us all experiences, some of them good, some bad, but regardless, life helps shape us into the way we are.

I wrote this book for those who enjoy crime thrillers, but readers of any genre are welcome. I hope you all enjoy this book and feel the creeping chill down your spine! Happy reading, *cluefinders*!

PART 1

CHAPTER 1

THE NIGHTMARE BEGINS

I clutched my gray raincoat tightly with my fingertips. Quickly scanning over the growing amount of people, I felt myself becoming more frustrated as minutes passed. The supermarket was not very crowded, so I had some space to sit down at the tables next to the hot food bar by the produce section. The tantalizing smell of freshly made sesame chicken and pork fried rice was almost too tempting to disregard, but I ignored my growling belly. There was work to be done first.

Damn it! He's not even here. Crap!

I shuddered, thinking of making small talk with that bastard. But I knew I had to get him to trust me.

Perhaps if I walked around the supermarket heading into the spice section for a bit, I could find him sooner than later.

I kept my head down to keep a low profile, but before I could even begin searching for the doctor, I found myself colliding with the person I was hoping to see all this time. It was my lucky day, after all.

It was him—short black curly hair, small Harry Potter glasses, lightly tanned skin, 5'5" tall, a prominent Adam's apple, and a few wrinkles on his face. His clean and gentle facade was hiding his true nature well. He was wearing dark blue scrubs. Doctor Jonathan Morgan was right in front of my eyes.

"Oh, my goodness! I am so sorry about that. I swear I didn't even see you," I said. "I was just in a rush to get some fresh groceries before they close for the night. I apologize again for crashing into you!"

He stood up and offered me a hand.

"May I help you, miss?" he said.

"No, thank you. I do not need your help."

"Oh, all right. That's fine," he said.

I immediately noticed the doctor's face turn serious. *Stupid Sasha. What are you doing?* I slowly stood up and dusted myself off from the floor.

"No, please. Please forgive me. I've had a rough day today, but that is no reason to be rude to you, Doctor."

I took off my sunglasses and smiled at the doctor. We stepped aside as people passed by.

"Oh, Sasha, I'm so sorry I didn't recognize you," he said.

"No, no. That's all right, Dr. Morgan. I didn't either, and I had sunglasses on."

"Still, Sasha, that was impolite of me, and if you don't mind me asking, how are you holding up?"

I struggled not to blurt out a snarky comeback.

"Ooh, I am a ... a ... I'm fine. I stopped crying a few weeks ago, but I still feel sad at night, but I find it easier to distract myself during the day. You know what they say. Time heals all wounds."

I glared softly at the doctor, secretly relishing his uncomfortable glance at me.

"Yes, well, time does heal all our wounds, especially loss. You just need some time to heal gradually to move on with your life."

"One can only hope things can truly be enough to get over. Isn't that true, doctor?"

"That is true," he said.

"Anyway, enough of this sad talk. I think we could just get a cup of coffee. What do you say, Dr. Morgan?"

He smiled and winked at me. "Call me Jonathan. And I say sure, why not?"

"Great, Dr ... I mean Jonathan."

He chuckled. "Would you like to accompany me for lunch this afternoon once I finish hitting the grocery store?"

I smiled as brightly as I could for him. "I would like that very much, Jonathan."

"I have a feeling I am going to enjoy getting to know you tremendously."

"Oh, you have no idea."

CHAPTER 2

A DAY IN THE LIFE OF SASHA

———

As I stretched my muscles and zombie crawled out of bed, I rubbed my eyes, coaxing them to wake up fully. I walked downstairs into the kitchen, pulled out a box of cereal, and poured it into a bowl with some oat milk. As I settled into my feast, I turned on one of my favorite podcasts, where I heard about yet another fascinating scenario based on a real-life crime, where they reveal the killer at the end. After breakfast, I followed my regular yoga routine and then showered to get ready for the day.

Upon finishing, I dressed up, gathered my gun, and headed out to my car before driving to my office in suburban Winston-Salem, North Carolina. I know you're wondering to hear about what happened next after my encounter with Dr. Jonathan Morgan at the supermarket and why I was waiting for him, but I promise you will know why soon, and no, we aren't dating!

I entered the small office—three desks, a cooler, and a kitchenette in the corner—and made my way to the desk at the far-right wall.

Ray was my colleague, my partner in crime. Or, rather, my partner-in-law, since we were both private detectives, operating out of the same small two-story building. Once I opened the lightly beige-colored doors, Ray hopped off his desk chair, greeted me with a soft smile with his pink lips, spiky dark brown hair, and James Bond–style clothes, and held a coffee cup in his hands.

"Morning, Sasha. Here's your green tea with almond milk."

I took it gratefully before taking a small sip.

"Thanks, Ray. But you know you don't always have to keep bringing me tea."

"Aw, it's no trouble, Sash. You know they say you should always spoil a lady first thing in the morning, so she's willing to lay with you in the sack."

Ray winked at me before I playfully shoved him away.

"Shut up, perv. Mmm." I took another sip before sitting down at my desk, starting my desktop computer, and sorting through files.

"Anyone come in yet?"

"Just one. This sweet old lady asked us to help find her missing neighbor and his bird."

I turned to look at Ray behind me. My eyebrows raised up.

"Are you serious? We don't work finding animals. We find and investigate humans only. You know that, Ray."

He stood up and walked over to my office, holding up his hands with caution.

"Now, now, just hear me out. She's seventy-six years old, all her kids live far away, they only see her once in a blue moon, and she met this bird around a year and a half ago after it got hit by a car. She's really good friends with this neighbor, Jonie, whose bird likes old lady Viola too—the lady who is asking us to find the bird, apparently. She's lonely and has only those two. Honestly, she reminds me of my grandma. She used to love animals too."

I felt my heart warm at that. He never really seemed like a sentimental person before.

"Does she have any leads on the neighbor's disappearance?"

Ray shook his head no.

"Uh, no, she claims they usually go to play bingo down at the center, and the bird goes too."

"Why? Who brings an animal—"

"I don't know! I don't know. But come on, have a heart for a little sweet old lady."

"Uh, sure, why not? If they mean that much to her, then fine. But you are catching it. I'm not a bird person. I'm looking for the neighbor."

"Ha ha, it's funny you should say that because she's coming back in like five or ten minutes."

Ray began to rub the back of his hand. I dropped my files and stood up, directly facing him.

"What?"

"Don't kill the messenger, but she wants us to help find it."

"Argh! Ray! I'm gonna kill you, I swear to—"

"Sash! It's only for a bit."

Ding! Ding! A short, gray-haired lady with slightly baggy clothes arrived in the office.

"Haa—hello? I was just here a moment ago. I spoke to a nice gentleman named Ray about my neighbor and his pet bird. His name is Lucio, and my neighbor's name is Jonie."

Ray immediately came over to her.

"Uh, yes, ma'am. That's me, Ray," he said as he turned to me. "And this is Sasha Thomas, my boss and colleague. Sasha, this is Viola Fabre. The bird and Jonie have been missing for about two days, and she would appreciate our assistance."

I stood up and offered her my hand. She shook it gently. Her hand was warm and slightly wet.

"Of course, Ms. Fabre. We will be happy to help in any way we can. Can you tell us the last place you saw them?"

"Oh yes, dear. We went down to the senior center, and when we walked outside, Lucio flew up in a tree at the park, and I didn't see him come down. When I offered to help Jonie, he refused and said he would take care of it, but the next day and the next, he hasn't been home."

Ray and I looked at each other in confusion.

"Uh, ma'am, may I ask what you mean by the bird not coming down?" I said.

"He never came down. He just flew up to the bird's nest and never came down, and then I thought I saw him flying over the harbor, but I can't be sure. I just want to make sure they are okay and can come hom—home." Viola's voice became sad and withdrawn.

I nodded to her and gently reached for her hand, giving it a small squeeze.

"We hear you, ma'am, and I can personally promise you we'll help you any way we can."

Viola smiled widely at me and squeezed my hands back.

"Oh, thank you. Thank you. Thank you, my dear. May God bless you always."

I smiled at her and turned to Ray.

"Well, Ray, it looks like we have another case to solve. So, shall we get started?"

Ray's nod and a tiny smile touched my heart briefly.

"We shall. Let's head down to the center."

Ray then got out a magnifying glass in his drawer and placed it close to his eye, exemplifying its immediate growth.

CHAPTER 3

WE NEED TO STICK TOGETHER

———

"Damn it, Sasha!" said Naomi as she paced around the basement of my house. "After everything you've told us about him, I can't believe you are reconsidering this!"

She flung her pool cue across the room, nearly hitting the window.

"Naomi, you know what I mean! We can't just jump into this! We have to plan the perfect way to bring Morgan down." I rubbed my temples.

"The bastard," I mumbled under my breath.

"Sasha! Sweetie, we already planned it out. We all agreed on you getting close to Morgan and gaining his trust. Then we can infiltrate ourselves into his life. You remember what he made us go through, right? The utter fact he fucking killed our children in cold blood should be enough for you!" said Max as he threw his half-empty beer to the floor.

The three of us had been meeting up at my place a couple of times a week for the last few months. We'd met at a support group for grieving parents and parents of children who were terminally ill back in May, and since then, Naomi and Max had become my closest confidants, my friends. They, too, had suffered at the hands of Morgan after being hospitalized and left in his care, and now that we had proof, they too were hungry for his blood.

"I get that. Don't you think I know that! I just do not want to cause that bastard to have a growth in his pants due to a few kind words and 'friendly touches.'" I put my fingers in air quotes as I felt a cold shiver run inside my body as I remembered the smug, nasty face of the slimy doctor.

Max gently placed his hands on my shoulders, giving me a kind look. His softness surprised me since he usually yelled at me the first chance he got.

"Look, Sasha. It's okay. I know you don't want to be around the doctor. Neither do I if I tell you the truth. But we both want this whole thing to be over. You know we have to do this. To get justice for our children, who we thought would be well cared for by someone we trusted to help them. Instead, he did the unthinkable. Sash, we can't just let that happen," he said with tears in his eyes.

"I know that, Max, but I—"

"But nothing, Sasha. You, more than anyone, should know our kids didn't deserve what happened. They should have gotten a chance to have a good life. But they did not get that opportunity, thanks to Morgan."

Shaking my head at them, I slowly closed my eyes and recalled the pain of having to inform Naomi and Max of Morgan's true nature.

***

"I'm sorry, my love. I'm so sorry, but I will not stop," I said, as more tears flowed and wouldn't stop.

One of my favorite photos of Jackson was with his bright cheeky smile, reddish-brown hair, and favorite zebra-striped shirt. I was sitting down on the living room floor, surrounded by dozens of photos of my son. My head was spinning as I downed nearly an entire bottle of tequila.

"I'm sorry, baby boy. I'm sorry I couldn't save you."

Jackson's eyes were piercing daggers at me. There was no way I could avoid his big shining eyes the more I tried to wipe my tears away.

"I promise you. I will make sure—"

Ding dong! Ding dong! The sound of the door immediately caught my attention. I knew it was them. I had invited Naomi and Max over to play pool and to tell them Morgan killed their children.

Looking at me expectantly, Naomi uttered, "So, what is it? What do you have to tell us?"

I won't admit I wasn't surprised by her question, but I had to push it all aside to tell them the truth. They deserved to know.

"Won't you both please come in? Want some coffee, water?"

"No, thank you, Sasha. But, what is going on?" Max chimed in.

"Sit down, please," as I gestured to my blue loveseat. The both of you—"

"Sasha! Quit avoiding the question! Will you please cut the courtesy crap already?"

With a sigh, I shook my head. "Damn, I can never get anything past you Nay, could I?"

With a sad look directed at both of them, I felt my stomach begin to heat up.

"All right then, remember our good doctor friend, Jonathan Morgan?"

"Yeah," they said in confused unison.

"Well, umm … He is not who you think he is." Max looked completely bewildered.

"What do you mean? He's not a doctor?" he asked.

"No, he is. Just a bad one." They both cocked their heads to the side.

"Let me start over. I recently discovered a file that said Morgan had purposely kept intimate images of small children, especially of his patients …"

***

When I opened my eyes, I saw Max standing in front of me.

"Max is right, Sasha," said Naomi. "Morgan is the only one responsible for the death of our kids.

"Sasha, he fucking choked my little girl!" Max said as his face twisted and his eyes got wet.

"I—I—know b-b-b but I …"

"What? What could you possibly have to say to that? Have you not thought about our kids? All we suffered?

"Of course, I have Nay. Morgan was terrible. It's just that—"

"Or do you just want to forget about little Jackson and all he went through?"

At that moment, all bets were off. I immediately stood up to Naomi and, without thinking about it, I slapped her across the face, ignoring her shocked gasp. No one mentions my son ever, no one. I didn't care if we were acquaintances. No one ever implies I didn't love my son!

"Never ever say that again about Jackson! He was everything to me. I want more than anything to avenge his and all the kids' deaths, but we have to be smart about this. But I am not a murderer. Understand?"

In my growing rage, I grabbed her arm and jerked her around.

"I just asked you a question. Do you understand what I'm saying?"

Naomi nodded while holding her cheek. Max automatically stood between us and held his arms out.

"Now, now. Let's all just calm down and take a deep breath. We can talk more about this later when we are all more relaxed. Agreed?" Max said in a stern tone, looking between Naomi and me.

"I can do that, can you?" I glared at Naomi.

"Me too. But don't you ever hit me again. Or else you won't get the passive side of me. Got it?" Naomi stepped closer to me.

"Yeah, whatever," I grabbed a pool cue from the floor.

"Little bitch," I muttered under my breath.

Naomi sent me a death stare. Max rubbed her shoulder.

"Sasha, sweetie …"

"I'll shut up."

"There now. Let's just grab some more beers and just have some fun, all right?" said Max as he picked up his beer and raised it to his lips.

"Sure, and I won't chicken out this time. I'll be stronger with Morgan, but who wants some more pizza?" Peering through the corner of my eye, I noticed Naomi's squinted eyes and angry huff at me. I nodded to Max.

"Yeah, I do, Max."

"Same here."

Max began calling the pizza place and, as Naomi walked over to the couch, I grabbed her wrist and pulled her to me.

"Listen here, Naomi. I don't want any problems here, but don't mention my son again. You have no idea what he went through, especially during the last few months of his life. Now, I care about you a great deal, but we can't move forward in this plan if we are going to be enemies or push each other's buttons."

Naomi shrugged off my hand and leaned in closer to me.

"I don't think I'm the one who's going to have issues when it comes to emotions, Sasha. I wouldn't underestimate me. You aren't the only one who lost someone, you rude ass bitch, so I'd watch it. You have no idea what I'm capable of."

Rolling my eyes at her threat, I said, "Watch it, Nay. I'm a private detective, and I can find shit out a lot faster than you can, so I'd watch it."

"If you think I'm gonna just—"

"Okay, pizza's been ordered, ladies!" Max's loud voice broke us out of our mini conflict. "I hope everything's cool here now?" He gestured to Naomi and me.

Smiling at him, I wrapped an arm around Naomi.

"Oh, we are great! Right, Nay?"

She stared at me for a few moments before smiling back at Max and wrapped an arm around me as well.

"Definitely, you know we have to work together to get this asshole," Naomi grinned at me.

I nodded. "Of course."

CHAPTER 4

THE CALL

———

North Carolina's sun rays beamed on my hands. House after house passed my sight, car after car, and tree after tree looked so peaceful that my eyes started feeling heavy and droopy the longer we stayed in traffic, trapped in our seats. I was driving to my office after getting some lunch at a new Thai place around forty minutes away with Ray.

"Damn it! I don't think we are going to make it back to the office as soon as we thought," I said. Ray and I were stuck on Interstate 73 for over thirty minutes.

"Ay, I know, Sasha. But it's cool since we are our own bosses, right?" said Ray as he began laughing and shaking his head at me.

I shrugged at just what was so funny about a sudden traffic jam, but whatever made him not be an ass in the car, I was happy with it.

"I guess, but we could have new clients calling at this moment, Ray."

"Sasha, remember they can call our cells, so just relax or take a chill pill. But you know we have other ways to pass the time as long as we are here," said Ray as he stuck his tongue out at me.

I rolled my eyes at that so fast.

"You are so disgusting. You realize that?"

"Eh, what's a guy to do as he is next to a beautiful woman?" He puckered his eyes big, sucked in his teeth, and eyed me up and down, then said, "I mean, you're cute too, Sasha."

"Not in your worst days, idiot."

"You don't know what you're missing, Sasha. But that's why I'm your friend and coworker. We connect well together."

"Whatever, Ray." My phone vibrated. I immediately placed the car in parking mode which was relatively easy, since we wouldn't be moving anywhere for a while since we were still stuck in traffic.

"Thomas."

"Hello, is this Detective Sasha Thomas?" said a strange voice I believed to be female.

"Yes, who is this?"

"Detective Thomas, we have your son Jackson Thomas here in the emergency room at St. Mary's Hospital with a head laceration from a fainting spell he had earlier today in gym class."

I immediately straightened myself up from my seat away from my previous slouch, ignoring Ray's looks of confusion and occasional taps on my shoulder.

"What? Is he all right? Please tell me he is okay. Tell me!"

"Ma'am, your son is under the best of care from our doctors, and he is at St. Mary's ER."

My shoulders were shaking so hard, it was getting so hard to breathe, and I felt a big lump in my throat.

"Yes, of course. I—I—I am on my way. Thank you," as I put the car into drive and hung the phone.

"Sash, what's happening? What's going on? Hey, talk to me. What's going on?"

"Just … shut up, Ray, please!" as I noticed the cars moving in order for us to move.

"Wait, Sasha. Take a deep breath and calm down." He placed his hands on the steering wheel.

Through my foggy mind, I discovered Ray and I had both hands on the steering wheel and I hit him in his side in an effort to push him away, but he wouldn't budge.

"Hey! Let go, Ray! We need to go to the hospital right now!"

"Which we will, but slowly and calmly!"

"Let go! Damn you!"

"Sasha, relax! Relax! Sasha! Sasha, look out!" as Ray made a sudden gasp. I looked back at him and found myself hit by a white puffy object.

I felt an abrupt tingle in one of my legs that briefly stopped before stinging again.

I woke up with a jolt, drool hanging off my lips, and feeling my phone vibrate as I recognized I was sitting at my desk, dreaming of that horrible day again. It will never leave my memory as long as I live. A constant nightmare, and I would have to talk to the one man who caused it. I answered his phone call.

"Hello, Dr. Morgan …"

CHAPTER 5

THE INEVITABLE ARRIVES

—

I buried my head inside my knees and reached my arm out in search of an ice-cold tequila glass. Once my hand found the glass, my drink momentarily burned my throat before I closed my eyes to remember the nightmare that was Jackson's future demise.

***

My heart was thumping back and forth as I shook my leg up and down. Ray put his hand on my shoulder.

After our car crash, medics rushed Ray and me to the emergency room but thankfully, we had little to no injuries, just a few scars on our hands and legs.

Once we were in the clear, I rushed up to Jackson's floor in the pediatric unit. Surrounding us were just white walls, shiny bright lights, occasional beeping, doctors and nurses running back and forth.

"Now, now, Sasha. Don't worry. I'm sure he will be fine," said Ray.

"Shut up. He's not your son, and you don't know anything."

"Sasha, I was a babysitter all throughout high school. I know just as much about kids as you do."

I shot Ray a glare. He raised his hands above his head in surrender.

"Hey, I'm just saying. Jackson's a strong kid. He's never let anything beat him. He's probably just got the flu or a stomach bug. It's no biggie. I used to get colds and viruses all the time too."

"Not my kid. I'm his mother. I know something bigger's going on here. I can feel it. He's not like the other kids. He never gets sick," I said.

"Sash, I just meant—"

The pediatrician suddenly arrived holding a clipboard. He was standing next to another doctor dressed in blue. His name tag said "Dr. Jonathan Morgan." He gave off this sort of young doctor type.

"Sasha Thomas?" Dr. Morgan said. A tall, dark-haired man with a small smile holding a clipboard in blue scrubs and a white coat suddenly stood a few feet away from Ray and me. His presence was unsettling.

I stood up to him.

"Yes, that's me. How is my son, doctor?"

"Hello, I'm Dr. Jonathan Morgan, I was the doctor taking your son's case. He's stable for now."

"Please, doctor, how is he? He's okay. Please, tell me, doctor, please!" My heartbeat was faster now.

Dr. Morgan pulled his surgical mask down and frowned at me. "Ms. Thomas, Jackson is stable. When he arrived in the ER, he had developed some heavy bleeding in his pancreas. We managed to stop the bleeding, but his pancreas is still hypoechoic, and because he lost so much blood, his liver is failing."

"What does that mean? Hypoechoic," I asked.

Dr. Morgan gave me a sympathetic look and pursed his lips.

"Hypoechoic means he has mass tissue in his body. It first started growing excessively in his pancreas. He then began to bleed heavily, and then it started spreading to his liver. We discovered he has Stage 3 cancer."

"Oh, God. How is that possible? He had no symptoms. He was perfectly healthy. How can he have cancer?"

"I understand. However, sometimes cancer can be harder to detect in children."

"Is there any way to help him? Chemo? Radiation? Anything? Anything at all?"

"Ms. Thomas, we can begin treatment by giving him one to two rounds of chemo immediately. I know it seems a bit too fast, but our tests show his liver seems to be failing because of the cancer.

Tears streaming down my face, my heart plummeted into my stomach, my hands went numb. I felt my shoulders going cold. Ray pulled me close and wrapped his arms around me.

"Shh, Sasha, it's going to be fine. He's in God's hands," said Ray.

"No, no, not my baby, no. Not Jackie, no, please God help me," I sobbed through my tears.

Doctor Morgan stepped closer to me and placed a hand on my shoulder, briefly patting it before pursing his lips together and nodding understandably.

"Sasha, if I may. There is an option that may be able to save Jackson's life. I can't promise any miracles, but I don't think it would hurt to try and see about this."

I lifted my head from Ray's chest.

"Waa—what—what? "What option is there?"

Taking a deep breath, he said, "We can give him something called ricin. It's highly potent but can be quite effective. We can give him weekly dosages of those. We can still give him chemo and radiation, and if we see improvement, then we can stop with the chemo entirely."

My stomach felt like it was in knots, pounding against my ribs, sucking in a breath. I felt nauseous.

"Oh, I—I don't know. Maybe I should find a second opinion."

"Sasha, it's a better option than what we have now. I mean, no offense, but Jackson isn't doing too good here," said Ray.

Still looking at the doctor, I said, "will he suffer?"

"No, I will make sure he doesn't. I promise you, he is in good hands," said Dr. Morgan.

With uncertainty shaking my voice, I said, "Oh—ok then. Let's give it a shot."

With a smile now plastered on his face, I suddenly felt a sharp knot in my stomach getting tighter by the minute.

"I know you would agree, Sasha. It's the best thing for Jackson."

***

Opening my eyes and clenching my hands into tight fists, I pulled out my phone and opened a photo of Jackson. As tears fell out of my eyes, a fire raged throughout my body as I recalled being an idiot and even trusting Morgan in the first place.

He was going to pay severely.

CHAPTER 6

LEARNING THE TRUTH

———

Green, green, and greener surrounded my vision. I was at a nearby pond not far from the office, seeing various frogs and ducks swimming close to one another. Holding a few pieces of white bread in my hand and throwing them a few feet away from me, ducks began to come close in search of the holy grail.

"Ribbit! Ribbit!"

"Quack! Quack!"

A small slimy frog came up and practically poked a piece of bread before moving on from it. Furrowing my eyebrows, it surprised me. Staring at the near crystal-clear water, I zoned out the longer I saw it.

"Hmm, isn't it amazing how no matter what issues happen, what anger or fear you feel, waves will continue going back and forth, and its residents don't need to work? They eat, sleep, pee, and can take care of their babies without any doctors, chemo, or any other crap? What I wouldn't give to be a frog."

Glistening, wet eyes that stung the more the water stayed in my vision.

***

Ray placed his hand, rubbing his thumb on top of my palm to comfort me. Previously, we were in the office having a slow day, barely any calls and only two people arrived requesting our services, so it was perfect for our little endeavor.

"Sasha, it happened a few months ago. You can't live life in anger or resentment. You need to forgive Morgan for what happened. Jackson would want you to," said Ray, who constantly called himself my right-hand man.

We were now in the hospital records room.

"Shut up, Ray. I need to do this," as I shuffled back and forth between a few blank and empty envelopes, as I opened drawer after drawer, not even looking at him.

"You can't even see anything in here." Ray paced back and forth while rubbing his elbows together. He was right. Except for a small light it was nearly pitch black.

"Duh, idiot. No one can know we are here." I opened another desk and searched for Jackson's name. Right then and there, it seemed as though we were lucky.

"Jackpot! Found it!" I did not hesitate to look through the contents of it. My blood went cold, and my entire body went stiff.

"No, he couldn't have …"

I continued looking through the file and read through names I didn't recognize.

My heart stopped when I saw the sentence, "Due to previous successful experiences with ricin for cancer patients, Dr. Morgan treated patient Jackson Thomas with multiple doses of …"

"Did he put something else in the …" Ray came up from behind me and grabbed the envelope from my hands before I even saw it.

"You know this isn't right, and Jackson would want you to be okay without him. That's why he picked you to be his mama because he knew you were strong and had a whole lot of love in your heart."

"But it was…"

"But nothing, Sasha. This is a hospital. You give private detectives a bad rep," said Ray as he continued holding the envelopes and placed them on a small counter in front of us.

At that moment, I felt pure fire start at my throat and tighten in my chest until I almost couldn't breathe. I pulled back fast from Ray and placed the files behind me.

"No."

Ray's right eyebrow went up in surprise, but I wouldn't surrender.

"Sasha, please."

I moved away from Ray and took a step toward the door. The hospital records room only had one light bulb on, making it hard to see my surroundings.

"No! Ray! I found my proof, and I will be damned if I allow your filthy hands to get rid of it," as I stuffed the file inside of my bag.

I walked over to the door before I felt Ray place his hand on my shoulder.

"And what is it exactly that you found in there?"

I turned over to see his eyebrows scrunched together. I sucked in a breath but gave him a one-sided hug.

"That is, I'm sorry to say, for certain people and me to know and for you to find out later. Thank you and have a good night," I said to Ray as I checked through the small window to see no one in the hallway, softly opened the door, and walked back to my car.

***

"Ribbit! Ribbit!

"Quack! Quack!" Hungry and demanding ducks requested my attention for more bread. I pulled out a Ziploc bag from my purse and crumbled more bread for them.

"Aah, easy life you live. You probably never even know the concept of revenge. You greedy bastards."

More ducks came back for food from a stranger like me.

PART 2

CHAPTER 7

MEANING OF LIFE

——

"No! No! No! No, no, no!"

I now felt a stinging pain in my right foot the more I kicked the metal garbage can.

"Why? Why? Why? Why? Why did you take him?"

I turned to look at the crucifix right above me.

"Why did you take him, God? Why did you take my boy from me?"

Raising my fingers to my hair, I clutched my head close.

I was in the hospital church. Dr. Morgan had announced to me my boy was dead. Various stained-glass photos of a baby Jesus, the Virgin Mary, and God illuminating an almost rainbow around. Perhaps the hospital meant the decoration to appear that way to give people hope for their loved ones, but I didn't care at the moment.

"Sasha, I'm so sorry, but Jackson had an adverse reaction to the ricin. He started hemorrhaging internally, and it caused his liver to fail completely. I'm so sorry to have to tell you this, but we lost him, Sasha," Morgan said a while ago.

"We lost him, Sasha."

"We lost him, Sasha."

My knees fell to the ground as I buried my head inside my hands. My throat was sore and drier than the desert. It was seeking a scotch, water, or maybe even a damn smoke. Rage filled my body at remembering how much ricin Morgan used on Jackson.

A tiny bit, my ass.

"Why? Why did you do this to me?"

My eyes burned the more I blinked. A tear quickly relieved me. The relief didn't last long, and soon I found myself crying buckets of water.

I close my eyes and see Jane's dark brunette hair with light brown highlights, her shining green eyes, and winning smile that always made me weak at the knees. She is hugging Jackson. He looks up at her; she ruffles his thick hair and sticks her tongue at him. The more I see them together, the more I feel pressure in my chest. It's time to be with them, I know it. Jackson and Jane deserve …

***

"Sasha," a voice interrupted my thinking. "Sasha."

I ignored it.

"Sasha."

I felt a lava-hot hand on my shoulder. It was so hot I flinched away because it was hotter than a frying pan.

"Jesus Christ!" I said, "What the hell are you doing?"

I turned around to see Naomi crouched down next to me with a sad look on her face. I huffed at her. She was giving me a pitying look. I hate pity. It's worse than anger. She hugged me tightly.

"I'm so sorry about Jackson. I had such high hopes he would make it through this. If you want, we can go to group this week, and you can talk about your pain and let us heal you and even provide some comfort to parents who are about to or have already lost their kids. But you know you aren't to blame. Jackson loved you, and I'm sure you've heard things about Dr. Morgan."

"Oh, you bet I have, ha!"

I raised my head up to look at Naomi. I felt my insides go aflame at hearing her praise for that monster. I could just kill her right now. Could I snap her neck right now so she'd shut up and get away with it?

"Morgan did something to my son. I just know it."

Naomi's look of understanding was so rich.

"How do you know?" she asked.

"I looked into him. He OD'd on the amounts of ricin, a drug commonly used to kill cancer cells. I saw it on the fucking monitor! I also wanted to know more about the treatments he so profoundly emphasized would make a difference, so I did some research on my own."

Opening my coat pocket, I pulled out an envelope composed of a few details of info I found explaining Morgan's ricin levels in Jackson and handed it to Naomi. Her eyes were red, and I could have sworn I saw fire beyond them. To my surprise, she pulled out a file and handed it to my hesitant hands. I started immediately shaking as I opened it. The file presented documents of the appropriate dosages of ricin, depending on the patient's size, age, and many more factors. My eyes bulged out the more I read. I couldn't believe it. We both had files based on the monster Morgan was.

"There you have it, Nay. Ricin is highly dangerous, especially for small children. Morgan clearly knew what he was doing. I know this file probably isn't sufficient, but I figured a voice confession might boost the jail time. Open your eyes, Nay—he is not the nice doctor you think he is. He is a cold-blooded killer!"

Naomi's blank face sent knives to my heart.

"This is just further proof he did this to my Blake." Naomi looked pissed at that moment.

"I don't know."

"You do. You know the truth." Naomi sat down across from me on one of the church benches and pushed me hard. She pushed me again.

"I'm not sure, but Morgan's file shows he injected over three kids, including my Jackson, with ricin. I'm not sure the amount of dosage, but I wouldn't doubt his role in Blake's death."

"Let's figure it out. We can search for more files," said Naomi.

Huffing slightly, "It's not easy to just break in and steal files. I mean, I need to find another excuse to go back in there," I said.

"I could give two fucks. Just find out the truth about what happened to my kid and call me when you do. He tricked me and so many more others. This bastard isn't going to make any more families suffer," Naomi said as she walked away from me.

"Then what the hell do you suggest I do next, Nay?"

She turned around to look at me.

"Seduce him, kiss him, sneak back in the room. I don't know, Sasha! He's a stupid man. You can fool him! He's a fucking idiot!"

"No, he's not, and actually, I have thought about …"

Naomi slowly turned around and looked at me. "Sasha, whatever the hell you got planned. Count me in."

"You sure, Nay? I mean, this isn't going to be easy and—"

Naomi flew right into my face, eyes unwavering and a tone unfaltering.

"Sasha, whatever it is. Count me the fuck in."

CHAPTER 8

ANIMOSITY HAS NO PLACE FOR COMPANIONSHIP

———

"Touchdown!" Max slammed down his beer on my coffee table in joy over a stupid football game. No offense to football fans.

"Oh, damn!"

"Ugh, what's even happening? I'm so confused!"

Two annoyed faces looked back at me. I shrugged in return.

"I don't know shit about football or any other kind of sports. So, sue me, assholes."

Max and Naomi were at my place watching a football game. The three of us were on the couch drinking sparkling water and munching on some popcorn. Naomi laughed.

"Ha ha, whatever, man. Just know I have one question." Naomi held up a glass bottle of San Pellegrino and started shaking it. "Uh, why is there no liquor? Why are we just drinking water? I mean, I can appreciate the bubbles, but ..."

She continued to shake the bottle. I grinned at her.

"Woman, I need to know more about football, and I need you as two sober teachers."

Nay rolled her eyes at me before putting the bottle down and laying back on the couch. "Whatever."

"Shh! Shut it. The game is on!" Max's eyes stuck to the screen as he waved his arms, trying to beckon us to be quiet.

Nay playfully shoved him back while I threw popcorn at him, which he could not catch in his mouth.

"Aw, fuck! I almost had it!"

"Uh, no, you didn't. I wasn't throwing it so you'd catch it. I threw it to your face so you'd stop being annoying."

With a gasp, Max held a hand to his chest.

"Who, me? I'm only ever annoying to those I deem who need to be annoyed as hell."

Max then placed his hands to his face and nodded repeatedly. Once again, Nay rolled her eyes, and I threw another popcorn kernel at Max. We continued to watch the game, which—according to Max and Nay—was between the Wake Forest Demon Deacons and North Carolina Wesleyan Battling Bishops, not that I knew of either. After a while, I tired of watching the game, so I decided to turn things up a notch.

"Hey, you know what? Why don't we sing karaoke?" Nay's and Max's looks of surprise made me giggle.

"Um, are you serious?" Naomi's confused voice asked me.

"Nay, why wouldn't I be serious? I have a karaoke machine from an old gift Jane gave me, and it still works even after these last few years."

Nay's eyes widened after hearing my suggestion.

"Ah, why not, Max?"

"I'm game, although I warn you I have an excellent singing voice."

"Pff! Yeah, right, I'm sure your shower has an outstanding validation of reviews," Naomi said to Ray.

"Whatever, let's do this, people."

I went into my room, opened the closet, pulled out a box, and found an old dusty karaoke machine, and I stepped out to show Max and Nay.

"I found it!"

Nay immediately went searching for my liquor cabinet.

"Sasha, if we are going to do this, then I will definitely need a drink."

I rolled my eyes at her and said, "blah, blah, blah, I hope it doesn't damage your vocal cords, Nay."

"Ha ha, we'll see about it, woman."

"Bring it!"

I immediately flicked the button to turn on the microphone. I switched to a karaoke app on my iPhone and chose the best song. I knew it would liberate me from my emotions. Ruffling my hair, unbuttoning my shirt to show some cleavage, and jumping on the table, I sang to my heart's content. Max and Nay's jaw-dropping faces didn't fail at making me laugh, but if I wanted to beat them, I turned around so they wouldn't cause me to fail. Upon finishing the song, I took a bow and stuck the middle finger at them.

"There's a lot that would surprise you about me, fuckers!" Naomi broke out of her trance, walked up to me, and grabbed the mic from me.

"Oh, you just watch, little girl," her voice amplified her confidence and microphone.

CHAPTER 9

THE PLAN IS IN ACTION

———

"I want to thank you for meeting me for lunch today, Sasha. I really appreciate you making this effort to make friends with me." Morgan held up his glass of wine to me.

"Ahh, well, you know, as a detective, I barely get enough time to get in some nutrition." I called him up to emphasize my anticipation to get together soon and catch up. Admittedly, the small "Michael's Café" with its "world-famous lasagna" with hot pink colors was cool. According to the owner, Michael, his father had passed down the place, and he worked hard to make it an authentic soul food joint. Posters of various dishes filled the room, but the environment had soothing, gentle music.

Oh, why, why did I think I could bear a meal with this asshole? Scrunching up a smile to the best of my ability, I grinned a bit at him, hoping he wouldn't notice my discomfort. Taking multiple sips of wine and overlooking my surroundings gave me a bit of relief.

"Of course, Sasha, that is perfectly understandable. No worries." Morgan suddenly reached out and laid his slimy hand on top of mine.

At that moment, my blood boiled, and I balled my hands into fists. My head felt so hot I could have sworn my face was redder than a strawberry. My stomach was in knots, and my mouth was dry as I imagined my balled-up fist punching Morgan.

Aah, that's it. Maybe I could just give him a tiny ta—no, stop it, Sasha! You will get your revenge soon!

Grimacing softly, I took a sip of water. I blinked fast as my mind ran through miles trying to think of the right things to say.

Opening my mouth slowly with piercing eyes, I said, "Yes, Jackson would want me to take care of myself. You, as a doctor, should emphasize one's health, right, Dr. Morgan?"

He blinked rapidly, raised his eyebrows, cleared his nasty throat, and wiped off his sweaty brows.

"Uh, yes, of course. Sasha, how many times do I have to remind you to call me Jonathan?"

He then gently squeezed my hand. I immediately pulled away.

"Ah, I'm sorry, Jonathan. I just …" He shut me up with a wave of his hand and shook his head.

"Don't worry about it, Sasha. Our friendship will go as slow as you wish."

I squinted my eyes so hard at that. I wanted to roll my eyes at that moment.

"Thanks. I appreciate that."

"Of course, all comes in due time. Maybe even more than a friendship? He gestures his hands out in a jazz hands manner, shrugging off the apparent rejection in my face. I opened my mouth to tell him off. "I'm just kidding, Sash. Don't kill me." Hearing Morgan's hearty laugh … I wanted to punch his throat.

"Ha ha, ha ha, in your dreams, Jonathan. I may kill you first, hmm?" Raising a glass of wine at him, smirking, and raising my eyebrows, I felt rough butterflies hit my stomach. I hoped he didn't hear the truth in my voice.

"Hmm, we shall see, Sasha."

"Salud!"

"Cheers!"

"Clink!"

Ah, this is going to be rich! The best part is this murderer won't even know what hit him.

We continued dining together, and I sucked in breaths to resist the urge to throw up every time this creep smiled at me.

All in due time, Sasha, I thought, mentally telling myself repeatedly. It was all in due time.

CHAPTER 10

TAKING A STEP CLOSER TO HER

"Ugh! Damn! I'm beat."

My sore muscles are completely draining and dragging me down. My eyes had heavy dark bags. I felt extremely exhausted after meeting with Morgan. I stretched my arms out, hearing a brief *crackle*.

Later that night, I walked into my bathroom and opened the tub to run a nice bath, pulling out my rose bubble bath. I undressed and pulled out my silky soft robe. As I returned to my bedroom and fished out my pajamas for the night, my fingers met a tiny velvet object. Once I pulled it out, I opened the box and saw a glistening, bright platinum diamond ring.

My cheeks felt wet as I held the ring in between my fingers. "Oh, damn it."

As I returned to the bathroom and laid down in the tub, I caressed the ring inside my palm. As my muscles relaxed and my brain shut off, I took a sip of wine and closed my eyes to go off to dreamland.

"Okay, Jane. We are almost there. Just a few more steps."

I was leading Jane blindfolded to her favorite place, Central Park in New York City. The "sudden trip" astonished her, and she giggled softly.

"Baby, how much longer? I'm getting impatient."

"Almost there, love. I promise."

Jane's hand in mine grew hotter by the minute. My stomach transformed into butterflies that repeatedly punched my insides the more nervous I got. I released her hand and removed her blindfold once we reached a stop.

"All right, babe. We're here."

Jane's eyes slowly opened, and her jaw dropped. It was a picnic for two, with plenty of sandwiches, her favorite champagne, and a big blanket to share. Jane put her hands in front of her face, squealed loudly, and lowered herself onto the blanket.

"Oh! Oh, my goodness, Sasha. This is so beautiful! Look at this! Ooh!" Jane raised her head and looked up at me. "Thank you so much, baby. This is amazing!"

I chuckled at her, leaned down, and gave her a soft peck on the lips.

"Of course, my love. You deserve the best. Now, let's just enjoy this." I pulled out two glasses, popped open the champagne, poured them into the glasses, and handed one to Jane.

"Ahem. I'd like to propose a toast. Jane, you have been my best friend for only four years, but it feels like I've known you forever. May we always be this happy and for every day to feel special, loving, and happy like this moment. Cheers."

Jane started tearing up.

"Cheers, baby."

"*Clink!*"

Tingly bubbles ran all over my throat, first creating a splash on my tongue.

We then opened the basket and dug into our lunch. I slipped my fingers into my pocket, aiming to hide the true surprise until the time was right. I specifically chose a secluded area with fewer people for more privacy so that it would be a moment just for us. Once we finished our lunch and held hands underneath the hot, scorching sun, my forehead began dropping bullets of water.

Jane noticed, asking worriedly, "Sasha, are you okay?"

I kissed her forehead.

"Yeah, no worries. All is good here. I just wanted to say something and do something, both of which are long overdue."

Jane's brows furrowed in confusion.

"What do you mean?"

I slowly untangled myself from Jane, hopped on one knee, and pulled out of my pocket the item I had tried my hardest to conceal from her. Jane's eyes teared up, and she held her hand to her chest.

"Sasha ..." she said in a low, hushed tone.

"I know I should have asked you this a long time ago, but here goes. I love you, Jane. I always have and always will. I promise to love you and to dedicate my life to making you happy and feeling like the queen you are. So, Jane Viotto, Will you marry me?" My hands started shaking the longer I held the ring box.

"Oh, my God. Yes. Yes, yes, yes!"

Jane was crying, and she leaned forward to hug me. I began crying over the sheer happiness I felt. My heart grew bigger over so much love. We kissed and cried together as I slipped the ring on her finger. Jane couldn't stop looking at it.

"Is this the promise ring you first gave me?"

I laughed at her question and nodded.

"Yes, because I love you. I decided to use the first ring I gave you to show how much our love has grown. It's a ring of promise, not just for marriage and a relationship, but a promise of commitment, love, and friendship until the day we die. I love you, Jane, and I always will."

Jane hugged me again.

"Oh, Sasha. I love you more."

I kissed my fiancée again.

Oh, Jane. I don't think that's even possible.

We kissed passionately again and laid down on the blanket again, staring up at the clouds.

"Hmm."

***

I opened my eyes and realized with a chill down my spine the bathwater grew cold. I still clutched the ring in my palm, and I kissed the stone softly. As I stood up and got out of the tub, Jane's smiling face returned to my mind. I held my prickly hand to my damp chest.

"I'm sorry I wasn't better for you, Jane. I love you, and I always will. Why did you leave? Why did you go away? Please come back. I love you, Jane. I'll be better, and that's a promise, baby."

Pressing a small kiss to the ring, I clutched it close to my chest, balled up in a fist.

CHAPTER 11

HITTING THE
BREAKING POINT

———

"Sasha, I've had such a great time tonight."

Morgan was so close to me as he walked me home from the restaurant tonight, I could almost feel his body heat. The night sky shone brightly with the stars. I felt a lump rise in my throat. I wanted to punch him or push him off, or maybe a bit of both. I shuddered. I realized Morgan noticed my reaction to his touch and thought it best to blame it on the wind. I placed my hands on my arms, shuddering at the chilly, imaginary breeze passing by.

Oh shit, Morgan noticed. The wind blowing toward us spread chill goosebumps toward my skin. Morgan noticed.

"Oh, no, Sasha, are you cold? Here, let me give you my coat." Morgan immediately slipped off his ugly brown jacket and put it on my shoulders.

"Ahh, wha ..."

My eyes were as big as saucers, almost like Bambi's. His hot palm placed on the back of my neck felt like fire on my skin.

"Get off me, Jonathan!"

Oh fuck, he may notice. My eyebrows reached my forehead.

"Uh, I'm so sorry, Jonathan. I'm just so ..."

"Hey, no worries. I should not have touched you like that."

"Thanks."

"No worries."

"I was a bit cold, though, so thank you for this."

We finally stopped walking once we reached my front door. Thank goodness. Seeing my welcome mat was such a relief from my tummy.

"It's my pleasure, Sasha. I'm a gentleman who will never allow a woman to be cold. I still open doors, pull out chairs, and pay the check. It's my motto to treat a lady right."

My eyes stung at how much I wanted to roll my eyes then. But I still wanted to turn up the fire.

"And that's why I am a gentlewoman. No one tells me what to do, but I appreciate being wined and dined."

"Ha ha, people wine and dine you for your work?"

"Oh, you'd be surprised."

"I understand. As a doctor, I always get an invite in the mail about this next big gala or from a hedge fund guy seeking surgery for this charity or his own thing for a trophy wife. They forget I'm a pediatric oncologist, not a plastic surgeon."

"Ha ha, wow, that sounds exciting."

Suddenly, an idea popped into my head.

He was going to get plenty of more excitement with me very soon. This was going to be quite delicious for this son of a bitch! I was going to throw him to the sharks by showing him exactly what he enjoys lying about: children.

"Aah, Jonathan?"

He stopped walking away and turned around to me. "Yes, Sasha?"

"When are you free again?" I asked before smiling.

"Early next week." He grinned and laughed softly.

"I'd like to see you again soon. I really appreciate your company."

"Well then, my lady, my company you shall receive. I'll pick you up at around eight, either next Thursday or Friday," Morgan said.

"Sounds great. Good night."

"Good night," Morgan walked away. Rolling my eyes, I leaned my head up against the front door.

Oh God, help me, please!

Briefly smashing my hand against the door, I realized I was in hell.

CHAPTER 12

KILLERS DON'T REFORM

———

"I'm glad you asked me to come with you to this park. It's so beautiful with the sunset, Sasha."

Morgan and I had been walking around a small park near my place. He was right. It was so beautiful. There was still a hint of the sun behind clouds, so we were okay to be out for a bit longer. Being in the park's atmosphere just felt so peaceful for the moment. We were initially going to my place, but I suggested the park so we would get some much-needed fresh air, mainly for me though not him.

"Yeah, I mean, you know. I used to take Jackson here occasionally. It was one of his favorite places."

My eyes started tearing up at the thought of seeing Jackson's face again in my mind. Morgan softly rubbed my shoulder.

"That's beautiful to hear, Sasha, but if this is too much for you, then we can go."

"No, it's fine. It's also nice to see a few happy faces running out and about. Wouldn't you agree, Jonathan?" I said to him.

Morgan's eyes widened like white dinner plates, and his hand reached around to scratch the back of his head.

"Uh, of course. I mean, who wouldn't want a child to be happy and healthy?" He uttered a nervous laugh.

"Right. And you would have experience being around kids. It's your job to make them happy and healthy even if sometimes things don't work out." Grinning at Morgan, I relished in his tiny nervous smile.

"Oh, of course, it is. Children are the most beautiful blessing, and it's my responsibility to take care of them. I try my hardest to."

"Ha ha, I have no doubt, Jonathan."

Morgan and I sat down on a swing set, watching many children run around, playing together. It was liberating, feeling the sun shining down on my face, blowing my hair. It was nostalgic as I recalled all the times Jackson ran in all of his fun and excitement.

"You know, when Jackson played here, he always said …"

"Ow!" A little girl slipped off the slide and scraped her knee. Her light blue eyes shed tears as her knee began bleeding heavily. "Mommy, I'm hurt! Waaaa! Waaaa!"

A tall, dirty-blond-haired woman ran faster than the speed of lightning and scooped up the crying little girl.

"Oh, no, no, no, my love. It's okay. It's okay," said the woman. She lifted the little girl's hair out of her face and gave her kisses on her forehead.

"Mama!"

"Mama!"

That was my son's voice. I turned my head to see Jackson on the floor, cradling his sore wrist after falling off the monkey bars. I ran to him, examined his wrist, and lifted him up into my arms. I kissed his shaking, chill body and carried him home like a delicate flower. He held on to me the entire night, not letting me go.

Morgan's voice brought me back to reality.

"You know, Sasha ... it's amazing how many children get hurt, get sick, and get put back together again. And this child fell hard, doesn't it just call to you how much she cries because she's suffering?"

At that strange remark, I stopped swinging but remained sitting on the swing and turned to look directly at Morgan. I furrowed my brows and squinted hard at him.

"What do you mean by that? Why would her crying call to me?"

Morgan stopped and clutched his stomach while widening his eyes.

"Oh, I just meant my heart breaks every time a child cries out or suffers. I guess that's why I became a doctor."

I cleared my throat.

"That's all."

"You are a good man, Jonathan." To further emphasize my point, I grabbed one end of the swing handles to move closer to him, reached over, and squeezed Morgan's hand while laying my other hand on his knee.

"Well, thank you, Sasha. It's getting late. I gotta run. Even in playgrounds like these, any time I get to spend time with you is a blessing."

"Aah, well. Don't you worry, Jonathan. I guarantee you will be seeing a lot more of me," I said to him.

I knew I needed to gain more information about him.

CHAPTER 13

JUMPING INTO THE WELL OF DR. JONATHAN MORGAN

———

A few weeks ago, after Ray and I found the file about Morgan keeping photos on his patients. After speaking with a few nurses, I finally managed to track down this mystery person. Allegedly, she had worked for several years as Morgan's head nurse, and he considered her family according to the hospital.

I had knocked into the front door of a dark brown home, hoping this individual would be here. I was lucky that within a few moments, the door opened.

"Yes?" A woman with grayish-white hair answered the door. She had a few wrinkles on her face and hands. She seemed to be around her late seventies.

"Hi, are you Amy Page?"

She squinted at me and nodded.

"Yes, may I ask who you are?"

"My name is Sasha Thomas, and I'm a private detective. I'm a friend of Jonathan Morgan. I understand you worked with him for a few years, from 2002 until 2004. I know it's been quite a few years, but I was hoping you could tell me a bit about him." She immediately frowned and placed a hand to her chest.

"Oh no! Is he in trouble?" She gasped.

"No, no, I am hoping to host a small gathering for him and just hoping to get some insight into his background, his likes, his dislikes, you know that kind of stuff."

She opened the door fully to me and asked me to come in.

"Oh, such a nice man, that Jonathan. Please come inside. Would you like some tea?"

"I'm good for now, thank you."

She gestured for me to sit next to her on the couch. I surveyed her living room. Plain colors of white, beige, and cream surrounded the environment. She had a small shrine of a man with wrinkles and white hair. I assumed it was her husband. Her home seemed quite well kept, very difficult to see any kind of dirt, dust, or even crinkle in sight. She must not even be a hoarder, which was strange for me. It was filled with pictures of small children in colors of black and white and even rainbows, hanging plates on the wall, and other objects around the room. She caught me looking at the happy smiles of the little boys.

"Aah, yes, my grandchildren. My boys are the light of my life. Do you have any kids?"

My stomach dropped at the question.

"Aah, I used to."

She frowned at my response.

"Used to?"

"Well, my … my son passed away a year ago. From cancer," I told her, omitting the actual cause of death.

Amy gave me a sympathetic look, reached out, and gently caressed my palm.

"Oh no! Well, don't you worry, my dear. I had a miscarriage a few months before I had my baby girl. There's always a second chance."

I smiled at her. I decided to change the subject.

"Anyway, what can you tell me about Jonathan? Any relatives I can invite to the gathering? Any allergies?"

She smiled at me.

"No, no allergies. He does love wine. Red wine, especially with fruit. He enjoys seafood, lobster in particular. I used to make him paella for his birthday, and he enjoys wearing suits, especially the color blue."

I nodded each time she spoke.

"Thank you. And any family or friends?"

"Well, he did talk about a grandma he missed a lot when we worked together. He called her his Nana. I remember he said her name was, I think Amelie Rose."

"Oh? He had a grandma? I don't think he ever mentioned a grandma to me," I said.

She smiled at me again.

"Oh yes, he adored her. His grandma and Jonathan were both August babies, and they always enjoyed getting ice cream with chocolate sprinkles for their birthdays. He said when he was about fifteen, she left home, and he's been looking for her ever since. His parents died young, and she was his only family. It broke his heart when she left and didn't even come back."

"Amelie Rose? Do you know if he ever found her? Or where they lived or what year she was born?"

"I don't, but I know she lived somewhere around Niagara Falls, and Jonathan used to travel from New York City to see her. She was around Montreal, I believe."

By then, I heard enough to start on. I stood and shook her hand.

"Thank you so much, Ms. Page. This has been super help-ful. But I think I've overstayed my welcome."

Amy shook her head and frowned.

"No, no, not at all, dear." She placed her other hand on top of our shook hands.

"Come back anytime." I smiled at her.

"Thank you so much."

For someone who appeared to love Morgan tremendously, Amy felt like a breath of fresh air. She was such a warm pres-ence. I could tell why Morgan liked her a lot. It was no wonder why her name was all over the files.

CHAPTER 14

BLISS DOESN'T LAST LONG

———

"Wakey, lovebug."

My eyes slightly opened to the blinding sun, welcoming me to wake up in my bedroom. I felt a few teeth gently nip at my ear. I recalled feeling something soft and cushy under my head.

"Mmm, that feels nice."

"Come on, sweetheart. Wake up."

"*No* ... I wanna stay in bed all day. Leave me *alone!*"

Jane's velvety laugh was sunshine to my ears.

"But sweetie, our son is getting up soon, and he would like his mommies to have breakfast with him."

My eyes transformed into large soccer balls. That didn't sound ... right? I sat up at that.

"Wha—wait, wait, wait, our son? We have a son?"

Jane's dazzling face scrunched in confusion.

"Of course we do, Sasha. Remember? Our beautiful boy Jackson? We adopted him almost a year ago?"

What the hell? I don't remember any of that?"

I put my hands on Jane's face, hoping she was real. She gave me a sweet kiss on my palms.

"Oh, you don't? Well, don't worry. I can make you remember little by little."

Jane's soft fingers began unbuttoning my pajama shirt. As she leaned in closer to me, I felt my cheeks burn and my body heat up.

"Mmh, I think I like the sound of that."

Giving my girl a nice big kiss, I pull her closer.

"Come here, woman."

My girl gave me a wider smile as she gently massaged my shoulders.

"Oh, you know I love it when you call me, woman."

We kissed passionately, and just before we could further place ourselves in pure happiness, bliss didn't last long. Suddenly, the door burst open.

"Mommy, Mama!" Wake up!"

Jane and I jolted apart. Jane murmured softly at me. Jackson jumped on the bed, shaking us away from each other.

"Come on, moms!"

Sighing deeply, "I told you he would get up."

"You did, but I just chose not to listen."

"That's why we love you."

Jane leaned in close, but Jackson fell in between us.

"Moms! Moms! Moms! I want bacon and eggs!"

Jane laughed before she shook her head.

"You always want that, kiddo." I looked at my boy. Jackson squinted his eyes at me.

"I need to eat, Mama!"

"Okay, kiddo. We'll get you some food. Hold your horses."

"Aah, you're wrong, Sasha. Bliss does last long as long as you put in the effort."

"You're right, my love."

We kissed again. This was bliss.

"Now, you need to get straight and get revenge on Morgan."

Wait for what?

Jane wouldn't mention revenge, ever. She was never the kind of person who believed in harming someone else, even if she was pissed. Scrunching my eyebrows together, I frowned at her.

"What?"

"Morgan killed Jackson. He deserves to pay, Sasha."

"No, he didn't. He's right here."

Jackson lifted his head up at me. "I'm not really here, Mama. I'm dead. I died because Dr. Morgan killed me."

"You need to make him pay for what he did."

"What, no!"

"Kill him, Sasha."

"Kill him, Mama."

"Kill him, Sasha."

"Kill him, Mama."

"No! No! Stop that!

"Stop saying that!"

"Kill him!"

"Kill him!

"Kill him!"

"Aah!"

***

I jerked awake. My room was pitch black. Jane and Jackson weren't there. Sweat completely drenched me.

"It was just a dream. They aren't here, and they never will be."

I turned around and looked at the time. It was 4:32 a.m. I tossed my legs over the bed, walked over to the bathroom, and splashed some water on my face. As I settled back into bed, I felt a plunge in my stomach, thinking of Morgan.

Damn it, Sasha, your family was right. You need to work harder to nail this son of a bitch. He deserves no mercy.

I then closed my eyes in a dreamless sleep.

"That's not true, Mama. We are still here."

"What the fuck? Aah!"

Jackson was standing by the bed.

"Mama, you know what you need to do."

"He's right, Sasha."

Jane was standing beside him, ruffling his hair. I couldn't believe they were both there.

"Morgan committed a crime, and he's got to pay."

"I don't know if I can do it. I have to get too close to him."

"Don't worry, Mama. You won't be alone. We will be with you every step of the way."

"Everything will be fine, my love."

I don't know how, but her soft but fierce words motivated me.

"You're both right. It will be fine."

"I will take charge, and Morgan will get a taste of his own medicine."

The last things I remember seeing before I fell asleep were Jane and Jackson's happy smiles. A longing dream that would never come true in one night. Lucky me, right?

CHAPTER 15

DREAMCATCHER
OF GOODWILL

———

La La La La! Idina Menzel's voice welcomed me to open my eyes. I quickly clutched my iPhone, hearing an anxious voice and heavy breathing. My eyes peered around the car's windows, seeing healthy trees, silently admiring the after-rain beauty of nature.

"Hello, this is Sasha from Sasha Thomas Private Investigator Services. How can I help you?"

"Oh um, hello dear. It's Viola. I just wanted to know how far you are to finding Lucio or Jonie. Have you found them yet, dear?"

We hadn't had much success finding them. Flyers and park visitors haven't been much help. However, Ray and I were giving it another try searching for the damn bird while driving around in Ray's car and then giving the Jonie search another round. I couldn't understand why but the damn bird kept reminding me of Jackson, his innocence, and how much joy they brought to those who loved them. If anything happened to it, I couldn't imagine telling Viola or Jonie.

"No, not yet. Mrs. Fabre. But I'm out trying to find him with Ray. We are in his vehicle, and I promise you, we should find them soon. We will let you know of any updates."

Ray raised his hands and nodded his head while munching on a leftover granola bar. We were below a few trees with a bit of shade, hoping to see the bird sometime soon.

"Hey, Mrs. F! Ray here!" His incessant chewing muffled his voice.

"Oh, thank you so much, dear. I hope you find him soon. Goodbye."

"Goodbye, Mrs. Fabre, talk to you soon."

I slid the call off and slipped my phone back into my pocket. I noticed as I rubbed my temples, Ray snickered at me. I shoved him, and he almost hit the driver's window.

"Hey! What's the problem?" I rolled my eyes at him. "Ugh! Must all guys be so gross and talk with their mouths full? I swear none of y'all have any manners."

Ray shrugged me off.

"Whatever, man. But how far are we getting with finding the bird and Jonie?"

I settled in further into my seat.

"Well, the residents said they saw a small green lovebird fly over to this area and sit up in that tree full of apples, and Jonie may have just gone to a friend's house nearby searching, but so far that's all we know so far," I said, as I pointed up at an apple tree hanging a few feet above Ray's silver-blue Cadillac.

In our previous exploration, the bird had not shown up yet, but we expected, thanks to the park residents, he would usually return before dusk.

"Mmm, well then it looks like we are gonna be here for a while."

Ray then found an apple to chew on. I eyed him in disgust with my lips curled and rolling my eyes. He noticed.

"What? I skipped breakfast. A man's gotta eat."

"No wonder why I don't go for guys like you."

"You do you, man. Want half?" Ray offered me a bite of his apple.

"I'm good, thanks. If I'm honest, I have no appetite right now, and the thought of eating even an apple makes me wanna puke."

Ray furrowed his brows and stopped chewing his apple.

"What's wrong? You good?"

"Yeah, it's probably just from the dream I had." I waved my hand to dismiss him.

"What dream? Did you have a nightmare or—"

"It had Jane and Jackson in it."

Ray's lips formed a silent "O," and he nodded slowly. "Oh."

"Yeah, oh."

"Well, do you know what caused it?"

My stomach went into knots once I heard that question. "I—you know I think it was just stress or anger. Sometimes, I don't know which is which. Just that this grieving shit hurts, and it's painful to get out of bed, the memories, all they do is just make me feel sad, and I wanna cry all over again."

Ray rubbed my shoulder.

"Sasha, you know you don't have to go through this all on your own, you know. That is not your fault, and you will make it through this, I promise you."

"I might not. I feel like I might explode with all of this anger and sadness I feel inside of me."

"Anger and sadness are components that can make us feel terrible, but they don't always last long. They can bring about pain, which can sometimes help us learn. It is proof of how much we loved someone and how much they loved us. Life can bring pain, but it's not forever."

"I feel like it is."

Ray gave me a sympathetic look where he pursed his lips tightly and sent me sad eyes.

"I know it feels like it is but believe me when I say there is a light at the end of the tunnel. As a matter of fact …" Ray reached out to his driver's rearview mirror and pulled out a small rainbow-colored dreamcatcher from it. "Here." He placed it in my hands.

"Ray, why are you giving this to me?"

"It's my favorite dreamcatcher. I think it'll help you sleep better. Legend has it they help catch the nightmares, so you'll only have good dreams from now on."

I raised my brow at him. "Hmm, you actually believe that?"

"Anything is possible, Sasha. Anything is possible," he said in a deeper voice that pushed me to believe how seriously he thinks I will dream better.

CHAPTER 16

HOW LOW CAN YOU GO?

———

"What the hell? You saw them? Jane and Jackson? Both? Together?"

Naomi's eyes widened the longer she stared at me. I nodded at her. We were in her apartment, particularly in her tiny living room. I had called her up to quickly go over the plan and talk about my dream. I had spent time with Ray prior. Ray and I spent the rest of the day waiting for a bird and searching for Viola Fabre's neighbor who we struggled to find, and then Ray dropped me off at Naomi's an hour later.

"Yes. Yes. Yes. And yes."

I stretched my arms out awkwardly, which was a challenge since she was seated so close to me on her red loveseat.

"What did they say to you?"

"They … They just … They told me to let Morgan have it. To let him have a taste of his own medicine."

"How do you feel about it?"

"I never wanted this, Nay. All I wanted was a family, a wife, and a kid. Morgan took that away from me, from you, from Max. But I never wanted this! I never wanted to hurt anyone! I just wanted a family!"

I slammed my hands hard on the brown coffee table in front of me. Naomi caught my hands.

"It just feels like I will never be happy, and all I get are just pure crap storms." Naomi's sad eyes nearly pierced into my soul. "Yup, just pure crap storms. Just one after the other."

"Sasha, you can't do that. I know you didn't ask for this situation. None of us did. But if you continue to feel like this, it won't do any good—not to you, not to your son, partner, our kids, nobody, not even Morgan. We know what he did. He's guilty, and he deserves to pay," said Naomi.

"Nay, we aren't killers. No sort of anger is worth taking a life." I sucked in a deep breath. "*Ever!*" I yelled almost to the top of my lungs.

"No one is saying we have to kill him or anyone else. We just need to make sure he doesn't do this to any more families, much less any more children. He's an asshole and perv. We know that. All you have to do is find the best way to incriminate him, and he's guilty and gone away for good. That's it, Sash. That's all you have to do. It's like what you said when Max and I first met you at the hospital, 'The more you love someone, the more pain you face,' and Morgan's the cause of our pain. You were right, Sasha, and it still applies. He is the spawn of hell."

Naomi's fingers pressed tightly, almost like a fist in front of her. They were becoming ghastly pale with a hint of red. I swallowed a sharp intake of air seeing her. She nerved me.

"Okay, Nay, you're right. That's all I need to do. I just need to—"

Beep! Beep! My iPhone informed me I had a message. My stomach became hot.

"Fuck! It's Morgan! We made dinner plans tonight. I told him to meet me here at the parking lot at seven—that's in five minutes. I suddenly felt hot and sick. I swear I could throw up or have a panic attack. Maybe both.

"I—I don't feel so good. Nay, I feel sick."

"Do you need a Tylenol?"

Naomi searched for a needle in a haystack in that rattrap she called a purse. I gently pushed her off.

"No, I'll be fine. I just need to drink some water and eat very little. God knows I can barely eat in front of that sleazeball."

Naomi placed her hands behind me, softly rubbing my back. On any given day, I would have smacked her upside the head, but for some reason, I felt comforted.

"You'll be fine. Just take a deep breath in and out. You're safe. Focus on your breathing. You're fine. You are fi—"

"Honk! Honk!"

Morgan's red chevy made me jump. I pulled back the living room window curtain and said Morgan had just arrived.

"Oh, great."

Naomi's hands stopped rubbing my back.

"You've got this, lady. You've got this."

I took a deep breath, said goodbye to her, and proceeded to go downstairs to that scuzzball, Morgan. He was wearing a nice light blue suit and navy blue pants. We had made plans for dinner that night, but the minute I sat down next to him, his slimy smile immediately made me gag.

"Sasha! How's it going?"

I had a strong urge to punch his throat. Mustering the fakest smile as possible, I swallowed a bite of anger at him.

"Fine, Jonathan. Thank you."

He smiled more at me. I resisted the urge to roll my eyes at him by sending him a soft smile.

"You're very welcome. I noticed you in a building nearby?"

"Oh yeah, I was just visiting a friend," Jonathan's eyes briefly squinted but shrugging at me.

"Okay, now where do you want to have dinner?"

"Oh, anywhere you want is fine."

"Great! I hope you like Indian. I know this nice place near the dog park." Morgan put the car in drive.

"Sounds good, Jonathan." I sighed and stared at the window as he began driving off to the restaurant. Oh boy, this should be fun …

CHAPTER 17

A BREAK IN THE CURTAIN

———

"Sasha, you are in for a treat! The food here is excellent." Morgan clapped his hands together before rubbing them together in excitement.

The smell of too many spices made my upset stomach not feel so good. In the background, I heard soft, peaceful music in the breeze, almost similar to the sound of wind chimes with some singer I had never heard of, and I couldn't understand the lyrics. The diversity of people in this restaurant was invigorating. I've never seen such a large melting pot.

"I'm sure I will, Jonathan. Thanks. I'm just not feeling too good. Stress, you know?" Jonathan's sympathetic look reminded me of when he was still treating Jackson.

"Aw, Sasha, but I wish you'd told me. We didn't have to go out."

"It's no biggie. I mean, who am I to pass up a free meal?"

Morgan started laughing heartily, which sickened me. It's not surprising he feigned compassion for someone who didn't feel the best, he did it to my son, and he just did it to me. Although I did have to admit the restaurant was absolutely gorgeous, combinations of red and burgundy brown and images of the Taj Mahal were all over the place but added a nice touch. This restaurant didn't seem overly fancy but definitely had a touch of elegance with sparkly lights around.

"Hello, there everyone! My name is Chad, and I will be your waiter tonight." Chad's booming voice startled me.

"Why don't we get started with a few specials or drinks?" Morgan immediately held up his menu and ordered us both mango lassis and veggie samosas. I didn't mind since I've never had Indian food and I wouldn't know what's the best to get.

Morgan then ordered us both a chicken tikka masala with a side of white rice which I hoped to God wouldn't upset my stomach further. But it wouldn't hurt since he's paying, right?

"Sasha, like I said, you are in for an absolute treat tonight."

"I hope so, Jonathan, because if I don't like the food, I'm not gonna hang out with you again." I winked at him. He laughed.

"Well, let's hope not because I would more than love to see you again." I forced myself to smile hard.

Dinner was a relatively quiet event. We were both satisfied with the meal, and my stomachache went away. I hardly felt the need to talk because, surprisingly, everything was delicious, and Morgan was just sending too many compliments my way.

Thank goodness for that. We finished early, and as I expected, Morgan paid the check, and after flashing Chad another nasty smile of his, he drove me home. We were just on our way back to my front door when suddenly …

"Mwah!" Morgan had suddenly leaned in toward me and kissed me. At that moment, I felt such absolute rage rise through me. How dare he?

"Slap!" I clutched my stinging red hand close to my chest. Morgan held his face while looking at me with tears on his face.

"What the hell is wrong with you, Morgan? How fucking dare you?"

"Sasha, I am truly sorry."

"Oh, you're sorry?"

"Yes, I am. I didn't think it would ..."

"Didn't think it would what? Be completely inappropriate? Be totally disgusting of you? Be completely uncalled for nor asked for?"

Morgan's sad eyes fueled my fire.

"You're right, Sasha. I should go. I understand if you no longer wish to see me any longer. I'll go."

I immediately remembered Naomi's words as angry and pissed off as I was. *He's an asshole and perv. We know that. But all you have to do is find the best way to seduce him so you can incriminate him, and he's guilty and gone away for good. That's it, Sash. That's all you have to do. All you have to do, all you have to do, all you have to do-do-do-do ...*

"Oh, damn it!" In my complete and total anger, I knew what I had to do. I had to avenge Jackson and those kids. They deserved it.

"Wait, Jonathan!"

He quickly stopped in his tracks and turned around to me. I immediately grabbed his hand and did the unspeakable. I grabbed his damn face and kissed him hard.

"Wait, Sasha, what are you doing?" Morgan pulled away from me. I knew I had a part to play. I might as well play the role as best I can.

"Jonathan, shut up." I swallowed my disgust, and we resumed kissing.

PART 3

PART 3

CHAPTER 18

THE KISS OF DEATH

———

Morgan's lips felt hard the more they pressed against mine. I felt his tongue gently requesting access to my mouth. I felt a knot tighten in my stomach the longer this kiss proceeded. I rejected him by closing my lips. From a distance, I could still smell a hint of his breath: cumin, oregano, and black pepper from the chicken he had earlier. It almost made me gag. His lips left mine and met my neck. I whimpered and shook my body. A hot wet tear fell on my face as I felt his lips rape my neck.

"Jonathan, please."

Morgan thought I wanted more, and he sucked my neck harder. The knot in my belly grew stronger. I slowly pushed him away.

"Jonathan, stop."

He slowly pulled away with a look of confusion in his eyes. I felt my breath slowly come in and out of me, the more I saw his eyes, cunning and charming, but also confused. He rested his hands gently on my shoulders.

"I … need to stop this. This is as far as we go tonight. Only this kiss, nothing more. I … I …"

"Sasha, you don't have to explain anything. I promise."

"I … I … do really like you, but I can't. I'm not ready."

"Don't worry, Sasha."

"Thank you, Jonathan. I guess this means good night."

Morgan nodded, but his head turned slightly to the left of me, his puppy dog eyes silently trying to implore me to change my mind. I knew I'd have to take it further, and soon. He could not wait much longer. Let him marinade in his desire some more. Morgan released my shoulders and smiled a little at me. He began to walk away.

"Good night, Sasha."

"Good night, Jonathan."

"Call me, John from now on." Morgan's repulsive wink may have seemed to him adorable and lovely, but it irked me more. I swallowed my bile and smiled largely at him.

"Good night … John."

I opened my front door and stepped inside. I instantly wiped my mouth, feeling my lips burn, but cool relief hit my mouth the moment sweet, ice-cold water stepped in to help. I immediately stuck my head under the faucet. My head stayed under the sink for a long time. Morgan's lips felt like sandpaper fresh from the garbage, and his breath reminded me of the inside of a dumpster. Don't ask how I know the inside of a dumpster. There are a lot of things private detective goes through for their clients.

My skin felt prickly and itchy. I needed to get rid of his taste and revolting smell. I immediately stripped off my clothes and hopped in the shower. I stood there, slipping down; the shame of knowing what I did and what I had to do soon irked my mind. The only images that constantly reappeared in my mind were Jackson and Jane's beaming faces. My skin felt sleet and shiny while my hair stuck to my face like a leech. Morgan took my family, and now, I had to prepare myself to sleep with him. How could I possibly do this?

Naomi's words echoed in my mind, "All you have to do is find the best way to seduce him so you can incriminate him, and he's guilty and gone away for good. That's it, Sash. That's all you have to do. All you have to do, all you have to do, all you have to do-do-do-do ..."

"All you have to do ..." the longer I thought of what Nay said, I don't know why I thought of telling her. She could "motivate" me again to go through with this plan. I rubbed my temples, but the longer I massaged myself, the more pain I felt all over my body.

"God, I hope this works." My stomach started knotting up the longer I heard Idina Menzel's *La La La!*

La! La! La! She picked up after the fourth sound.

"Sasha? What's up?"

"Nay, I—I—just tell me why I need to do this."

I walked over to the kitchen and opened up a bottle of wine. As the cork released a *pop*, I heard Naomi suck in a breath.

"You have a divine animal right to protect and avenge your offspring, and the moment you hold them, you know you would do anything because you love them. Morgan took it away. He's an asshole and a perv, and all you have to do is seduce him, and then he's gone away for good."

"I—I know... but he absolutely disgusts me."

"I understand how you feel, Sasha. But it takes time, and I promise you nothing will feel better than the moment you see Morgan taken away in handcuffs."

"Can you please just come over? Please, I need to tell you about tonight."

"What do you mean? What happened?"

I clutched the phone close to my head, hot tears going down my face the more I thought about it.

"He … He … He kissed me. At first, it really pissed me off, but I kissed him back. I just felt so nasty, he's evil, and his lips were on me."

I was now crying, and I could vaguely hear a humming sound from Nay's side.

"Don't cry, Sasha. I'll be on my way soon. I'll help you. It's all right."

Taking in a deep breath, I rose out of the tub.

CHAPTER 19

AN UNLIKELY ACQUAINTANCE

———

"I honestly don't really see the issue here, Sasha."

Naomi sat on my couch with a glass of wine in her hand. It had taken her twenty minutes to get to my living room, and we weren't getting far in our conversation. We were having another one of our deep talks at my place, almost like a girl's night. I called her back a few hours ago, asking her to come and chat—anything to blow my mind off this nasty kiss.

"Isn't this what we planned? Morgan feeling closer to you and you feeling closer to him, to trust and love you enough to admit what he's done?

Nay's confused face stands out with her frown lines, curly brown hair, and heavily squinted eyes.

"He makes my skin crawl! Just thinking of sleeping with him or kissing him makes me sick, Naomi. Can't you get that?"

She walked closer to me and put her hand on my shoulder.

"Sasha, I get it's terrible, but you need to forget about your own feelings in this. If you keep focusing on how disgusted you feel by him, you won't get far. You know I hate to say it, but you have to keep Jackson in the back of your head and think about the plan. I mean, if anything, you can always use toys with him."

I shuddered at that. My eyes went wide the moment she said that.

"Naomi, how can you possibly? How the hell? Who the fuck—"

"Sasha! You know it's a way of sleeping with him, so using a toy probably wouldn't be so bad. But why are you getting so wound up about this? I'm offering you a solution here."

Fire immediately built up inside of me. I stood up and walked over to the living room window overlooking the patio. I shook my head at her.

"You are a real dumbass. Do you know that? You are a true dumbass."

Naomi's face revealed she was livid with rage.

"Sasha! Calm down! You haven't even gone too far yet. I can prepare you for that, so you'll be fine. I thought sleeping with Max would be bad, but it's not."

My eyes widened.

"You slept with Max? You slut."

Naomi rolled her eyes and raised her hands above her head.

"Hey, I'm just saying, sex with someone you didn't expect isn't as bad as it sounds. Most of the time."

Laughter quickly fell out of my lips. "I can't believe this. I came to you seeking help, compassion, and understanding, but it's clear I'm not going to get that, especially not tonight. So, you know what?" I stood up from the couch and opened my front door.

Squeeze! The door's opening decided to make a loud announcement.

I looked over to Naomi.

"I need you to leave."

She looked at me in confusion.

"Sasha! I am here to help you."

"Well, clearly, you failed tonight. So, please just leave, now."

She stood up and headed out the door. Naomi looked pissed off with her furrowed lips, and she rolled her eyes again.

"I care about you, Sasha. But you need to stop wimping out on me."

"Thank you, Naomi. You have overstayed your welcome. Good night."

She left my house for the last time that night. Slamming the door, I still felt anger and loneliness rise inside me the more Naomi's words went through my brain.

"He's an asshole and perv, seduce him, and he can go away for good. All you have to do …"

All you have to do. The longer I thought of what Nay said, it made me think of talking to Ray. Fun, old smooth talker Ray. If I needed to do this, Ray had to know. He's dreadfully savvy in the art of flirtation. Reaching for my phone by the toilet, I knew I needed Ray.

La la la! There it was, Idina Menzel's voice returned. There was a nearby crackle.

"Hello?" Ray's sleepy voice alerted me.

"Ray? It's me, Sasha. I need to talk to you about something. Something really important."

CHAPTER 20

SHIT HITS THE FAN, LIFE GIVES YOU LEMONS, MAKE A FRIEND

———

Clutching the phone to my ear, I walked downstairs from my bedroom to the kitchen to brew some coffee and get my composure, all the while hoping Ray wouldn't judge.

"Ray, I have something to tell you."

"I mean, Sash, it's never a bad time for a booty call," he sounded tired, and there was no background noise. Have I woken him up? I couldn't worry about that.

Rolling my eyes slightly at him, I remembered why I called him. "Idiot, can you be serious for once?"

At my tone, Ray immediately stopped laughing. I guess he realized this was no regular conversation.

"Okay, okay. I'm sorry. What did you want to talk about?"

I felt my stomach drop. "It's really hard to discuss, but you were the only one I could think of right now."

"Okay, but I mean Sasha, it's kinda late, but—"

"I know. I know, but I needed to talk to someone, and you're the only person I knew I could trust."

"Okay, I'm wide awake now. Shoot. I'm all ears."

Taking a deep breath, I steadied myself and rose up to sit upon my bed. This was it—the moment of truth.

"Remember when we broke into Dr. Jonathan Morgan's office to steal his file on Jackson?"

"Yeah. What about it?"

"Well, I went and dug a little deeper, and it turns out Morgan not only used an excessive amount of a drug called ricin, but he also has quite a few closed cases against him from other patients.

"Wait, what?"

"Morgan had a few closed cases for negligent misconduct."

"What the hell? How many? What's ricin?"

"It's a highly potent toxin used carefully to help kill cancer cells, but Morgan used too much. He has over six cases, but apparently, he used a lot of influence and money to manipulate families into keeping quiet."

Crack! Crack! Ray's breathing peered through the phone. "Okay … so what does that mean?"

"He used too much ricin. Using too much of that crap or routinely abusing it can be deadly. He did it on purpose. He injected too much of that shit into Jackson so many times it killed him. It also means someone caught him before, but he just knew how to shut people up."

I heard Ray lift the covers as he shuffled himself out of bed. His voice suddenly nerved me, turning my stomach into knots. He cleared his throat but took a pause.

"Uh, Sasha. I—uh, do—do—do you have any proof?"

Without hesitation, I responded, "It's all in the file we found sneaking into the hospital records room."

"Okay, and have you gone to the police?"

The knot in my stomach grew even tighter hearing him say that.

"Umm, well, see that's the thing. I don't plan on going to the police, just not yet anyway. You see, I have a plan. Well, we have a plan ..."

"We? Who's we?"

"Two other parents who lost their kids to Morgan, Naomi and Max. Their kids also had cancer, and Morgan treated them."

"I see, and what's your plan? I mean, between the three of you."

My mouth suddenly went dry.

"We ... we ..." I said as I sighed. "We have a plan for me to seduce Morgan enough that we get him on video admitting his role in our kid's deaths and maybe get a bit of revenge on his face or goddamn limbs or maybe his favorite appendage."

"Sasha! Do you—do you hear yourself? Are you literally saying you're willing to kill or purposely harm this guy? A well-known doctor? A doctor, by the way, who has the power and network to destroy your reputation, especially if you are in prison?"

"That won't happen. We made sure of that, we specifically discussed this plan a thousand times and I've mastered it in my head, we won't get caught.

Ray stared at me for a long time and swallowed before taking a deep breath that strangely was loud enough for a FaceTime call.

"So, that's it? You're just going to go through with this and let this darken your soul? Sasha, I know you. You are not a killer, and you wouldn't harm anyone. I don't think this is a good idea. Just turn Jonathan in and forget about that asshole. He'll suffer tremendously behind bars and possibly as some big guy named Bubba's prison wife."

Tears started streaming down my face.

"You don't understand, Ray. Trust me, I don't wish to do this, but my rage toward this guy is too strong, especially after that nasty kiss we had tonight—"

"Whoa, whoa, whoa, you kissed him?"

"I didn't want to, but I realized it's part of the plan."

"Sasha, no, please. I'm begging you, don't do this. This isn't you, and this isn't right."

I was crying fully now.

"Ray, you don't understand. I don't want Morgan, and I never will, but he took my boy away when all I ever wanted was a family. He took that away from me, and now I will never get that back."

"Sasha, I understand, but I know you. I know you are better than this. You shouldn't force yourself to do something or someone against your will. It won't do good for you. You deserve to be happy, but this won't bring happiness. I can promise you it won't."

Ray's calm and gentle voice began to soothe me after tonight's fiasco.

"Sasha, you are a beautiful and strong human being who has survived through the world's worst hells that life has thrown at her. But you never let it stop you no matter how hard it got, and that's how you became a private detective and the most important role ever, Jackson's mom. I get you are pissed because of what Morgan did, but it's never too late to repent and do the right thing not only for you and your heart but for your son. You and I know he wouldn't want his mom to do something in the name of revenge. Jackson was your baby, and even though I don't have any kids, I know he would be proud and happy to have had you in his life, but he wouldn't want this for you, Sasha. Please consider not going through with this."

I sniffled.

"Oh, no, please don't cry, Sash. Please don't cry."

His words calmed me down. I guess there was a whole side of Ray I never knew. He always stood out to me as a gross and perverted jerk, but he was never this kind before without usually making a sexual joke.

"Thank you, Ray. Thank you so much. I appreciate this."

"I'm glad, Sasha. I don't want you to get hurt."

"Thank you, Ray," I said, sobbing into the phone. "I don't know why your words are making me feel better after tonight."

"You're welcome, Sasha, and I want you to continue feeling better. So, I'll tell you what, let's meet up at the Sunset Diner, the one a few blocks away from the office, for some breakfast or just coffee before work. Like around seven-thirty-ish? That way, you and I can keep on talking, and you can tell me, not about the plan, but about how you've been feeling because something's telling me you haven't had a chance to vent. Am I right?"

I felt such an urge to open up to him.

"You're right, Ray. I've felt so alone since they diagnosed Jackson." I sniffled again.

"It's going to be okay, Sasha. I promise you. Why don't you try getting some sleep? I'll be on the line until you catch some Z's. Lord knows you don't need any more bags under your eyes." Ray gently laughed.

It made me smile slightly and hiccup. I slowly stood up, walked over to my bedroom, and lifted the covers up before settling into them.

"Ray, ha ha." I hiccupped.

"That might help. I'll try getting some shut-eye," I said to Ray.

I slid down and held the phone before pressing the speaker button. I wiped my tears away and tucked myself in.

"Just get comfortable, Sasha. I'll sing to you."

My eyebrows reached my forehead at that.

"You? You sing?"

"Only a little bit. My audience is the rubber ducky and dust bunnies in the shower mostly."

"Eww! Ha ha!"

I laughed until my stomach hurt.

"Shut up, Sasha! He guffawed through the phone. Now, close your eyes and count the sheep. You're in for a treat."

Go to sleep.

Go to sleep.

Go to sleep and good night.

Count the sheep.

Count the sheep.

Close your eyes.

Close your eyes.

The longer Ray sang to me, I felt comforted as though he were giving me a warm hug through the phone. This felt … odd. I hadn't felt this secure and safe since Jane. As he lulled me to sleep, I felt a soft smile perch itself on my face.

CHAPTER 21

I GOTTA GO MY OWN WAY

———

As we'd agreed last night, I pulled up to Sunset Diner at twenty after seven, with a splitting headache and a rumbling stomach.

"I get that you are pissed because of what Morgan did but it's never too late to repent and do the right thing not only for you and your heart but for your son, who you and I know wouldn't want his mom to do something in the name of revenge especially for him."

I gripped the steering wheel so hard that my knuckles turned white. I knew Ray was trying to help but he didn't get it. He chose not to have kids. It was too easy for him to judge. But I knew what to do.

"Damn it, Ray! Why are you making me do this?"

Thump! Thump! Thump! Thump! Thump! I beat the shit out of my steering wheel.

Honk! Honk! Another car was behind mine

"Move, asshole!" I waved my left hand, letting him know to pass me.

"Bitch!"

As the idiot left the lane, I gave him the finger. I pulled up in front of the diner. It was your run-of-the-mill eatery, where Ray and I would occasionally grab coffee and bagels.

Ding! A bell went off as I entered. A cute, short, tanned redhead greeted me with a big smile as I walked closer to her. Under other circumstances, I would have asked for her number.

"Hey there! Table for one?" Her voice was so high. It was adorable.

"No, table for two. I'm meeting someone. But I don't mind having room for one more, maybe a table for three?" I gave her a wink.

Her cheeks got red. "Oh gosh. Really? Well, I'm working but maybe another ti—"

"Sasha! Over here!" Ray's booming voice and excited jumping flew in the corner of my eye.

Dang, Ray. Way to ruin some flirting. I looked back at the hostess.

"Well, that's me, beautiful. I guess another time then."

I laughed at her happy over nodding. I walked over to Ray and sat down in the booth across from him.

"Well, Ray. You sure know how to ruin a girl's good time."

He guffawed so hard at that. He wore a light blue jacket, dark blue shirt, and black pants. His hair was greased back with some cheap gel, perhaps.

"Sasha, I apologize, but we have more important things to do. Like talking one on one."

"I suppose you're right, but you know my reasons."

"Sash, I may understand why you feel like you need to do this, but you and I know this isn't right. You could murder him and become someone I don't even know."

"Why do you say that?"

Two menus faced us, and I found myself briefly scrolling through mine.

"It's true. I've seen how hard you try to get what you want, especially with our cases. It consumes you, and this is no different. You need to understand that ..."

"Hi there, my name is Amie. Can I take your order?" It was the same redhead from the restaurant's entrance.

"I'm good. Just a coffee, please. Sasha?"

"Just an iced coffee, thanks."

"Got it, two coffees. I'll bring them out to you shortly."

"Thanks."

"As I was saying, Sasha, you and I know this will eat you alive because you aren't for torture nor murder." He said in a lower voice while looking over our surroundings so no one would hear us.

"Ray, I never said I was going to kill him, but he deserves to pay."

"Sasha." Ray shook his head disapprovingly at me. "You know it's not what Jackson would have wanted."

Our waitress returned.

"All righty then here's one hot coffee and one iced coffee. We also have cream, milk, and sugar. Let me know if you would like anything else. Enjoy."

"Thanks." As I set up my coffee, Ray reached over and held my hand gently.

"I'm just saying, I care about you. I don't want you to get hurt or consumed by hatred. You're too good for that."

Smiling softly at him, I now remembered what I had to do. Ray was truly such a kind soul. I squeezed his hand back. I took a deep breath and licked my lips.

"You're right, Ray. It's not who I am. It's not who I want to be. It's not who I was. It's not who Jackson loved nor believed his mom was. I get it. But I've just been feeling so lonely and angry I couldn't find a way to get rid of the anger properly. I drank every night, emptying bottles of whiskey or tequila. Strange men and women were leaving my home before I woke up. It was a mess. It's all been such a blur, and it's not like Naomi and Max can understand. Their rage blinds them so much I've just become their errand girl or scapegoat."

Ray gave me a sympathetic smile and ran his thumb over my hand.

"I'm so, so sorry, Sasha. I wasn't there for you, and I should have been. I'm so sorry, but things are going to change. I promise you. From now on, we are hanging out more. We are doing TV and beer nights, flirting with women, getting breakfast and coffee together, the works. You don't need to feel this way, and you won't feel alone anymore. I'll even sing you to sleep every night. But you won't feel this way anymore. I can guarantee that."

"You don't need to do that." I slowly pulled my hand away from him.

"I know, but I want to. There's the difference. You matter, Sasha, and so do your feelings. No one should ever make you feel otherwise."

Ray's words were so beautiful they made me shed a tear. I hadn't talked to anyone about such private things for so long. Ray's warm and genuine support caught me off guard. It was always just about what I could do for others. Not what they can do for me.

"Ray, you truly are one of a kind, you know that?"

He shrugged at me and released my hand.

"Uh, I try. But let's drink our coffees and head to the office, shall we?"

"Yes."

We drank our coffees, and within thirty minutes, we were at the office on the corner of Eighth and Murray.

Hours went by, sitting by the computer, and then Ray said he was heading for his lunch break.

"I'm feeling pretty hungry. I think I want some ramen. Sasha, wanna come with?"

"No thanks, Ray. I'm okay," I was sitting down at my computer on Amazon trying to find new surveillance equipment to further spy on Morgan, a small device that could be placed somewhere in either his car or his home.

"You sure? Wouldn't kill you to go out for a bit."

"I'm good, really. Maybe just bring up a small soup or something." Ray eyed me suspiciously but shrugged.

"Okay, if you say so. I'll be back. Don't get into too much trouble."

"I won't,"

I rolled my eyes at that. Once the coast was clear, I pulled out my iPhone and dialed Morgan's number.

La! La! La! I felt my stomach drop the longer I waited for him to answer. I whispered, "This better be worth it."

Crackle!

"Hello?"

"Hi, Jonathan."

"Sasha! What a surprise! I thought I scared you away." I heard him laugh softly. The more he spoke, even after a few minutes, the more irritated I was.

"I guess you are looking for round two? Ha ha, I'm kidding."

I rolled my eyes at that.

"I guess you can say that. But I'm calling you to ask you out for lunch Friday afternoon. Is that cool?"

"Oh yes, I'd love to. Of course! Does noon work for you?"

"Yes, it does."

"Wanna meet at the Velvet Café?"

"Sounds great. They have an excellent chicken Francese."

"I'm excited to try that out. Thanks, Jonathan, see you then."

"See ya, talk to you soon," Morgan said back to me.

Beep! Beep! Beep! I put the phone down, set it aside, and rubbed my temples. Morgan had sent over a message, a happy face emoji.

"Grub time, Sasha! I have arrived!"

Ray came in and set down two huge bags of food. We chose to sit down by the office patio and dig in.

"Sasha, I can't tell you how happy I am that you're taking the path of no revenge. Truly, allowing yourself to heal and spend time with those who care about you will really make a difference. Thank you for allowing me to help you through this."

Ray continued to eat. I immediately felt so guilty.

"Me too, Ray. I think you're right," I lied.

CHAPTER 22

CONSPIRING WITH A SIDEKICK

———

I bundled up my coat, clutching it close to me. I was walking in the ice-cold snowy winter, aiming to meet a mysterious stranger. Someone who may help me get a step closer to learning why Morgan became who he is. I began to quicken my pace, impatient and dreadfully cold. The crunching of the snow kept me sane on the way.

Jesus, how much longer? I pulled out my iPhone and saw the location was around less than two minutes. Damn, I must have walked a lot already. My heart began to beat fast when I finally reached my destination: a shabby, black house that looked run down and beat. It looked unstable and horrendous. I double-checked to see it was the right place. Unfortunately, it was. I knocked on the door, and I received no response. I knocked again, and still no response. I knocked a third time before I heard a shrill.

"Who's there?"

"My name is Sasha Thomas. I'm an acquaintance of your grandson, Jonathan Morgan. I just wanted to ask you a few questions about him."

At my response, the door was opened a small crack but not fully, although I was able to see a bit of the elderly woman's wrinkly hand and small face.

"Why—why—why do you want to know about him? He can't find me. No, please, he can't find me! No! No!"

The woman began to shrink down in fear and was about to close the door. I immediately caught it before she could slam it shut.

"No, wait, please! Jonathan doesn't know I'm here. I promise you. He has no idea. I promise."

Amelie stared at me in shock.

"Can you just please tell me about what happened? What did he do?"

Amelie's eyes widened.

"What didn't he do? He had two sisters and an older brother who took part in making his life miserable. I used to tell him to ignore them, but he couldn't stand it. He had bullies in school who pantsed him, gave him wedgies, kicked him hard a lot, and life at home didn't help. His parents were always away at work, though I tried my best to comfort him. I could never prove it, but I felt like he had a hand in setting fire to his family home, killing his entire family. He always said he was in the library reading, and he didn't know until it was too late. Even when the biggest bully suddenly got blood poisoning apparently from this big bug that laid on him from a nap on school grounds."

I widened my eyes at that. Apparently, Morgan was really dangerous from the beginning.

"Oh wow, do you have any proof of that?"

She shook her head.

"No! I never could find it. But it always creeped me out whenever he would buy these tiny baby boy and baby girl dolls.

He would chop off their heads, or take apart their limbs, write nasty words on them, and stick them out like lawn ornaments. I tried to talk to him about it, but he was too far gone. Then I realized he was too attached to me. He would threaten to attack anyone who got close to me. One night when he was sleeping, he was about fifteen at the time, I decided to pack my stuff and leave. I never saw him again. He emancipated himself, and I've been hiding from him ever since. Now, I've said too much. If I spend any more time out here, he could find me. Now kindly leave, please!"

Amelie immediately tried to shut the door. I tried to hold off. Amelie's eyes widened in panic, and she attempted to shut the door forcefully with all her might. She was desperate to go back inside.

"Wait a minute!"

"No, please go!"

"Just tell me—" Fire was building up inside me. She knew so much and didn't want to open up. "Please, ma'am! I need your help!"

"Leave me alone!"

She rushed to close the door, but I immediately pushed a fist against the door and a foot under it to prevent her.

"Please, Amelie! Tell me!"

She paused before taking a deep breath and looking at me.

"All I can tell you is he is insane and to stay away from him as much as you can. Keep him away from children. He's always been strange with his affinity for them. Watching with his binoculars. Birds without wings. Said they couldn't fly away. So, please just stay away!"

She then shut the door on me. I was left reeling over everything she said.

CHAPTER 23

THE SHOW MUST GO ON

———

This snazzy café was cozy and seemed like the kind of place you could settle in during a stressful day. It was Friday, and there were so many people for a slow afternoon. I told Ray I was off doing some investigative work for a client, and I would be gone for most of the day.

Morgan and I were sitting outside. I ordered a shrimp salad, and for him, the damn chicken Francese he wouldn't shut up about. I decided I needed to twist things up a notch and decided to take Morgan up on his offer to dinner. To turn on the charm, I wore my best Italian Shoemakers high heels and a small skirt. I even shaved my legs. He wore his dark blue scrubs with some fancy jacket.

"Mmh, Sasha. I'm so glad you asked me out to lunch. I can't tell you how much I wanted to see you again. You are a very intriguing woman."

Ugh, this idiot. I could just tell he was trying to seduce me with his bewitching eyes and Cheshire cat-like grin. It nearly made my stomach turn into knots by how nauseous it made me. He ordered the best wine of the place, aiming to charm me with his knowledge of wine. While he paraded away like a wine snob, I could sense by his consistent smile he was more than relaxed.

"Sasha, I swear this Merlot is just amazing. I chose it because it reminds me of you, ageless and fine. You don't deserve to be bottled up and stressed out. It's nice to see you free and enjoying yourself."

"Thanks, Jonathan, I'm glad. The office can be stressful too." I went back to enjoying my salad as best I could.

"Sasha, would it be too forward if I asked to see you more often?"

My eyes went wide at that.

"Perhaps, Jonathan. Let's see how far we go first as friends."

"I understand. You just take your time."

"I appreciate that, Jonathan. I like having a chance to talk to you one-on-one and get to know you better. More than a doctor but as a human."

"Sasha, I truly appreciate your friendship. I want you to know I am not here to take advantage of you, and when you are ready, I hope you don't think I'm too forward if I were to ask you to go steady with me. But whenever you are ready, of course."

Taking a deep breath, I steadied myself aiming to throw my plate of food at him, but I remembered Max's words.

"He is not a good man and thinks he's so charming. But you can show him who's boss."

I had to show him who is the boss here while playing hard to get.

"Sure, Jonathan. But I hope you are a patient man. I mean, we all know who seeks what he wishes must not be greedy."

"Haha, don't you worry, Sasha. I will never be greedy with you. You are safe with me." He raised his glass of Pellegrino at me.

"Thanks, John. I'll hold you to that."

I raised my cup of wine at him while lifting my eyebrow suggestively at him and sending a wink his way.

"Salud."

"Cheers."

Clink!

PART 4

CHAPTER 24

LIVING A LIE

———

"Cheers, Sasha."

"Cheers, Ray."

It's Friday night. Morgan and I "enjoyed" our earlier lunch date. We made polite conversation, spoke about how "interested" we were to spend time together again, and made plans to go out to a bar and grill sometime soon. We didn't come up with an estimated date yet. He continued to "charm" me and paid for dinner, which I was secretly relieved for since I didn't want to pay too much for an overpriced chicken dish. Thank goodness we didn't schedule anything as of yet.

Ray and I were in my basement playing pool and drinking Heineken beers for the night. So far, I was winning.

"Sasha, I can't believe you're beating me. I'll have a comeback. You just watch." He made me grin impishly.

"Ha ha, yeah, right, loser."

"You just wait, Sasha."

Smack! Ping! He finally made a winning shot. I nodded at him and raised my eyebrows.

"Not bad, Ray. But you are gonna lose tonight."

"Ha ha, so how was tonight's client? Did you find any clues?"

Upon hearing that, my stomach dropped.

"Oh, you know. It was fine. I didn't find much, but I will try again soon. Today just wasn't the day, I guess." I lied.

"Aah, I gotcha. Need any help?"

"No, no, I'll be fine. But I would worry about maybe helping you lose even more tonight, especially right now."

I set up another round, placing the numbered balls together.

"Bring it on, woman!"

The rest of the evening was spent poking fun at one another and laughing. It felt different than with Nay and Max. It felt more natural. I didn't know why, but I felt like I could truly be one with Ray. Perhaps as more than a coworker or friend but more like family until I heard the sound.

Beep! Beep! Beep! Beep! That was strange, but I immediately recognized it as my iPhone getting a text notification. When I paused our game to look at it, I noticed it was Morgan.

He asked me, "Sasha! I had such a great time with you today. I was wondering if you would like to have dinner at this great seafood place called Le Bernardin next Saturday. Let me know what you think."

"Ugh, great."

Ray noticed my displeasure.

"Sasha, you okay?"

I looked up from my phone to him.

"Huh? Oh right, yeah, I'm fine. Just a damn spam message. No big deal."

Ray was skeptical as he squinted his eyes.

"You sure?"

"Yeah, of course. Let's just get back to playing. Shall we?"

Ray and I resumed our game for the night. It was all fun and games, providing me a few moments of bliss from all the strain and stress of Morgan and this dangerous situation I was placing myself in. I then pulled my iPhone out of my pocket and texted Morgan back, "Sure, looking forward to it!"

CHAPTER 25

THE LADY AND THE TRAMP

———

Morgan and I were having dinner at Le Bernardin, where he paid musicians to play a few songs next to our table. The atmosphere was beautiful. There was a string of lights hanging above us, resembling stars. On our table, we had a medium-sized dark green wine bottle with a candle placed on top of it, and painted flares of red, green, and white were all over the walls with black and white photos of Italy and the people there.

"Sasha, I hope you enjoyed the music. I felt it would add a nice touch in an Italian place, Italian music, Italian wine, Italian food, and a complete Italian presence."

I would admit it was nice, but it felt like the right thing but the wrong person. A small candle in a wine bottle shining brightly, illuminating a romantic setting. It made me tear up.

"I appreciate that, Jonathan. I've heard Le Bernardin is a really fancy place. I do appreciate the effort."

That statement wasn't a lie.

"You are worth the effort, Sasha. You deserve to be treated once in a while. This is totally my pleasure for a friend who's been so stressed out. I felt like you deserved the chance to relax. Now let's just enjoy our dinner. How's the wine?"

"It's good, Jonathan. Thanks."

"Of course, Sasha. I'm a doctor, but I still know how to treat a lady with style." He guffawed heavily.

We continued eating our pasta dishes. Until I had a sudden thought jump at my head and pulled out my iPhone and pressed "Audio recording." I took another sip of wine. I suddenly felt nature calling was me urgently. After delicately wiping my mouth with a napkin, I politely excused myself to the restroom.

"Excuse me, Jonathan. I need to go to the bathroom."

"No worries, Sasha. Take your time."

I walked over to the bathroom, and upon washing my hands in the sink, I noticed from a weightless pocket I had forgotten my phone at the table.

Oh shit! I hope I haven't gotten any messages. Or else I'm busted.

I immediately walked back to the table, hoping my racing heart would settle down. Upon reaching the table, Morgan's beaming face met me. I sent him a nervous smile. Thankfully, my phone was untouched in the same spot on our booth table.

"All good there?"

"Uh, yes. All good, I mean, except I left my phone behind. Not that I need it, but you never know if clients will call."

"I understand, but no, your phone didn't ring. But you did get a few dings."

I noticed I had a few messages from Ray, Nay, and Max. Just simple texts asking how I was doing from Ray and to destroy Morgan as best I could from my partners in crime. Feeling unsettled, I decided to change the subject and seduce Morgan as much as possible by getting to know him.

"So, Jonathan, doctor with style ... do you currently see a lot of patients?"

Morgan looked up from his pasta, furrowed his eyebrows, and widened his eyes.

"Uh, not usually, sometimes it depends on the day or how many appointments I have filled up, Sasha. Why do you ask?"

"Just curious. What's it like being a doctor? Especially for children? How does that feel like?"

"Well, to be honest with you, being a doctor is not always easy. I mean, it's what I have to do, and usually, the kids always end up healthier and happier, thanks to careful precision and cautious administration of medications and medicine."

"That's so admirable. You and so many other doctors do so much good for children, adults, and even animals. That's truly amazing." I lied. Morgan smiled softly at that.

"Thank you, Sasha."

"May I ask how long you've been a doctor?"

"For about a couple of years now, I was in med school for four years, three years in pediatric residency, and I think about nine years at this hospital."

My jaw dropped at that. He must have done this longer than I thought.

"Wow! That's a long time. I can't imagine staying that long for school or a career."

Morgan laughed heartily twice before answering me.

"Aah, it's no big deal. Being a doctor was always my passion. I was willing to spend as much time to make my dream come true."

"That's cool. Aside from being a doctor, do you have any hobbies? Do you like painting, hiking, cooking? For instance, I love swimming and taking walks in my spare time."

"I actually love going hiking. I try my hand in cooking sometimes, but I'm not the best."

"Ha ha! Me neither. I feel like I could even burn water if I tried." His eyes crinkled at the corner with laughter.

"I doubt you could ever burn water. I am curious to hear about you, Sasha. Where would you go on vacation if you could?"

With no hesitation, I answered. "Italy."

"I am a huge pasta lover, and I can't help but obsess over Italian villas."

"Italy does have some nice assets, especially women who ask a lot of questions." Morgan laughed again. I thought I found no humor in this particular comment, it won't do me any good to snub his joke, so I let out a giggle.

"I hear you, Johnny boy. But a girl can still ask questions, right? To truly know someone's heart, you get up in their grill. Ha ha." Silently praising myself for Morgan's small smile.

"I get you, Sasha. But as I said, you are safe with me, I promise."

"I better be, because like I said, you don't know what I'm capable of, buddy." I took another bite of food.

"I know, Sasha. Can I kiss you again?"

Disgust instantly rolled up in my belly, almost making me gag my food up.

"Yes, yes you may."

We both leaned forward against the table, and I mentally prepared myself for this while turning off my recording. This wasn't a moment I wanted to remember. Leaning in forward and pressing my lips close to Morgan's, I felt him smile before he pulled away.

"I gotta say, you are a great kisser, Sasha."

I grinned at him.

"Oh, you'd be surprised how many things I'm good at, Jonathan."

He winked at me before lowering his voice.

"Ah, I see. Well, I am definitely up for a treat."

CHAPTER 26

ADD FUEL TO THE FIRE

"Ugh!

I gargled a ton of mouthwash and spat out what remained in my mouth. I still felt Morgan's taste on my lips and my tongue. No matter how much I gargled, the taste of his chicken dish wouldn't go away. My mouth began to burn the more I added Listerine inside.

However, it did stand out to me how much pride Morgan had when answering my questions as though he believed he was a good doctor and tried to convince me otherwise. But I knew the kind of man he truly was, and he wouldn't fool me. My striking bathroom light felt like a furnace burning my soul, judging me for what happened that night.

"Ay!"

I planted myself inside of my upstairs bathroom for the past half hour. It became my sanctuary. I sucked my tongue inside. As I began to breathe in and out, I slowly put the toilet seat down and sat down on it. I put my head in between my hands, rocked back and forth, and started crying.

La! La! La! My iPhone was next to me on the sink. Once I picked it up, I saw it was Max.

"Hello?"

"Sasha? It's me, Max. I was just wondering about how your date went last night."

"How do you think it went? I played the game, and now my prize is nearly finishing up the Listerine bottle and getting another one. Hence my mouth burns. Morgan's tongue is slimy, and his mouth is disgustingly wet. Any more details there for you?"

"All right, all right, I get it. It was unpleasant. But … it's for a purpose and just relax. It's over now. Take a shower, kick back with a cold one, and go to bed. Sound good?"

"You have no idea. I just want this night to be over. But I will say Morgan definitely had a ton of confidence when he expressed how much he loves being a doctor, but I also made sure to get to know more of his background. But I will say, Max, he's had years of being a doctor. I have no doubt the list of victims goes on and on."

My blood boiled thinking of how many innocent kids Morgan targeted.

"Damn that asshole. I hear you, Sasha, and that's good. You're getting closer to the goal but before that. Let me ask you, have you spoken to her yet?"

At that question, I immediately felt anger rise from my chest.

"No, and I don't want to."

"Sasha, it's been a few days. She's grieving just as much as you. She doesn't deserve to be in the dark like this."

"I don't care. She's not my favorite person right now."

"I know, but you should talk to her soon."

"Don't force me, Max. You know she's willing to push me past my limits just for her own benefit. She doesn't care about me."

"Sash, she does. More than you know. I know she's not easy, but she's a grieving parent, just like you. She knows what you went through."

"You're right. I just need some time before I talk to her again. Don't push me, Max, okay?"

"Copy, Sasha, but just think about it."

"Fine, Max, good night."

"Night."

Beep! Beep! I just received a text notification from Morgan.

I slammed my iPhone down on the sink, put it in my pocket, and walked out of the bathroom. I tucked myself in bed and stared up at the ceiling. Even though I knew I was lying to him again, I knew only he could help comfort me and make me feel better after time with Morgan. I needed Ray, and I needed him now. I heard a crackle as I waited for him to answer.

"Hello?"

"Ray, it's me. Are you up?"

"Yeah, what's going on?"

"Everything's all right but can … can … can … can you sing to me again? I haven't had a good night. I feel like I had a nightmare. Can you please sing to me?"

"Of course, but will you tell me tomorrow?"

"I will, first thing tomorrow. But please sing to me?"

Go to sleep.

Go to sleep.

Go to sleep and good night.

Count the sheep.

Count the sheep.

Close your eyes.

Close your eyes …

My eyes grew heavy, and the last thing I remembered was hearing Ray's peaceful voice soothing me to sleep.

Go to sleep.

Go to sleep.

Go to sleep and good night …

CHAPTER 27

EXPLORING A
NEW HUMAN

The sudden rush of air that flowed around me as I opened the office door was strangely comforting. Ray's singing managed to soothe me to sleep, but my insomnia got the victory tonight. I took a shot of tequila, letting it burn my throat to comfort me back to sleep and make the tossing and turning sizzle out of my system. My surroundings were nearly dark thanks to my sunglasses, but I caught Ray grimacing, trying his best not to laugh out at my disordered state. Thankfully my practice was small, and it was only me and him who worked at the office. That tequila did not sit well with me this morning. But I had a responsibility, and we promised Viola we'd help her, and we did. The neighbor Jonie had forgotten his steps and was actually staying with his daughter, who is also looking for the bird, who still hasn't appeared.

"Ugh! Ray! Don't you dare laugh at me, or else you're dead!" Ray quickly noticed me and handed me a cup.

"What's this? I can't do coffee right now."

"I know, you're in one of your moods, and it's organic green tea with a splash of almond milk. Guaranteed to make you feel better in no time."

"Ay! You're a lifesaver, Ray."

He laughed and shrugged at me. "Ehh, I try to be. You know you can trust me. I'm always here for you."

"Yeah, I know, Ray. Thanks." I lowered my face, trying to avoid his gaze.

"Sasha, you all right?"

"I'm fine, Ray."

I started lowering all my bags and sat down at my desk. Ray walked over to me and sat on my table. He instantly grabbed one of my hands and began rubbing it.

"Sasha, whatever it is, you can tell me. I'm not here to judge you."

I sighed deeply before raising my head to meet his gaze.

"I know, Ray. But it's whatever. It doesn't matter."

"Apparently, it does, or else it wouldn't be upsetting you this much. Or why else have you been calling me in the middle of the night asking me to sing you to sleep when you know my voice sounds like a dying angel."

Just thinking of an angel dying made me laugh out loud. "You don't have a bad voice, Ray."

"Pff! Yeah right! Sash, you can admit it, I sound like a dead camel begging for water on Mars. You probably sound that way in the shower." I playfully shoved him back.

"Asshole, tsk."

"Anyway, what do you say we get outa this joint? Maybe get some fresh air and maybe get some grub while we're at it? Let's face it, we ain't doing much today. Let's seize the day. Hmm?"

I pursed my lips together and raised an eyebrow.

"Sure, why not?"

"Aah, that's the spirit, Sash. You won't regret it!"

I rolled my eyes at him.

"Uh, whatever. Let's just try to focus on work."

I turned my attention back at the computer, but with hungover eyes and a sleepy, pounding head, my attention was not for work. Maybe Ray was right. I did need a break. Screw work with a damn hangover! I slowly stood up and whistled at Ray.

"You know what? Screw work! This is my business, and I'm calling it for a day or an hour or whatever. Let's ditch this joint."

Ray smiled at me before gathering up his car keys.

"Let's do it."

CHAPTER 28

JUST BEING ALIVE

———

"Sash, don't worry about the cost. I've got it."

Ray shoved all attempts of mine to pay for lunch. We were standing in front of our favorite hot dog stand. Neither one of us felt like having a sit-down lunch that day. It was about a ten-minute walk but about a five-minute drive from the office, and it felt nice to get some sun on my face while feeling the wind blowing through my hair.

Screaming children filled the annual local street Carolina Fair. An abundance of colors, corny clown music, and occasional shooting sounds would pop up, making me jump. I have never been a person for arcades, carnival fairs, circuses, or anything like that, but Ray was kind enough to want to distract me from my troubles, so I appreciated his efforts.

"Oh, come on, Ray. It's not okay for you to pay for all this."

"Sash, just relax and enjoy this meal. Also, it's part of the rule, I invited you, and so, I pay the bill."

"But …"

Ray raised his hand up to silence me.

"I'll tell you what, next time we go out to eat together, it's your treat. But right now, it's mine, so let's just eat. We can sit at a park bench, and then we'll go back to the office."

"I'd like that, thanks, Raymond."

He grinned at that. "Hey, hey, hey. What's with the "Raymond?" It's just "Ray here, ha ha."

"Okay, okay, Raymond," I said with a teasing voice.

"What do you call a pig with a black belt," I asked him.

"What?"

"A pork chop!" I joyfully yelled.

I held my stomach the longer I felt pain, but this pain was different. It was pleasurable and had a pinch of happiness attached. We watched several people walk by us, but it didn't matter. I was enjoying myself. Ray was an actual funny dude, to my surprise.

"Ay, Ray, why are your jokes so corny, but they make me laugh anyway?"

"Because everyone finds joy in the little things they see, hear, and touch. Plus, you have a good laugh, Sasha. You deserve to let it out, woman."

"You make it sound so easy, Ray, but—"

"Excuse me. I'm getting a call."

My phone rang, and I took it out to see Morgan's name on the screen.

"Aren't you gonna answer it?"

I quickly placed it on silent so he wouldn't disturb me any longer.

"No, it's just spam. Let's just sit here for a bit."

My face went low as my eyes hit the floor. Ray noticed and tapped my knee.

"Sasha, what's wrong? You okay?"

"Yeah, I'm fine. I haven't laughed like this for so long."

I couldn't remember the last time I laughed that hard. Even then, I struggled with being happy and living in the moment. Ray squinted his eyes at me.

"I don't believe that, Sasha. Tell me what's wrong."

"I'm fine, honestly."

"I still don't believe you, but I'm here for you whenever you need me."

"Thanks, Ray,"

"Sasha, would I be too forward to ask if I can hug you? It's okay if not."

"I don't know what to say to that, Ray."

He grabbed my hands and gently squeezed them.

"It's up to you, only you. You have the right to say no." It touched me that Ray was a genuine person, unlike Morgan. My heart grew three times larger with an appreciation for him.

"You may, Ray."

"Are you sure?"

"Yes." Ray slowly leaned in, opened his arms, and gave me a big hug. My body went through a major tingle from my head to my toes.

"Thank you for allowing me to do that, Sasha. I appreciate you letting me hug you."

"Thanks, Ray. I'm aware since hugs aren't really my thing, but it's okay. I'm glad you recognize that."

"Would you like to hang out later tonight? There's a traveling carnival not too far from the office. It will only be in town for a few days. I'd like you to explore it and have fun before they leave."

I smiled and squeezed Ray's hands back, which were still holding me tenderly.

"I'd love to, Ray. It would be a pleasure."

Ray caressed my hands again.

"No, Sash. The pleasure would be all mine."

My smile began to burn my cheeks.

CHAPTER 29

FORGETTING THE PLAN

"Step up! Step right up! To the balloon and darts! Winners get prizes! Step up! Step right up!"

The announcer yelled through the speaker. He was aiming to gather a few victims of his own. Ray and I walked through the bright flashing rainbow lights of the carnival. There was an array of screaming, excited children, strong whiffs of food odors, funnel cake, hot dogs, French fries, chicken tenders, and much more. Shining, bright colors constantly surrounded my vision.

It had been a slow workday, and we had no cases, so we decided to close early and spend some more time together. It was an added benefit being the owner and the boss of my own business.

"Ray. I know you said we were going to relax and hang out but is this what you meant by chilling? I mean, not that I mind, but this seems corny."

"Come on, Sasha. Give it a chance. You can hang out, walk around, play some games, but most important: eat!"

"Ha ha, I can see that, but there's a bit to think of. We don't have kids, nor are we, and the food here is just a bunch of junk."

"Oh, come on Senorita Sourpuss. Live a little, eat, drink, and be merry! I recommend you try the Whac-A-Mole first. It helps get a lot of the frustration out, trust me."

Ray motioned for me right in front of the game.

"Tempting, but no thanks."

"Oh, come on. It's fun. Try it."

Ray handed me a paddle, inserted in formerly quarters transformed tokens, and pressed play. Immediately, the lights turned red. Ray stood behind me and pressed down to smash the randomly appearing moles. His touch was warm, and it brought tingles down my spine. The minute I began smashing moles upside their damn heads, I started to visualize Morgan's head with his tongue teasing me to hit him.

"Come on, Sasha! Come get me!"

"Oh, I will. Pop back up, asshole! Come on, asshole! Die asshole!"

The moles were too fast, but I managed to smash on a few of them.

"Bam! Bam! Bam! Bam!"

I felt Ray's arms jerking me back to reality.

"Whoa, Sasha, you okay?"

"Yeah, why?"

"Well, you started calling the moles assholes and started pounding on them hard."

"I did? Huh, well then, you're right. It lets out a lot of frustration."

I dropped the mole-smacking paddle. I noticed an entire line of tickets heading our way as a reward for my excellent round. I guess that's something I can thank Morgan for. Dealing with him for the last few weeks triggered such anger in me that I needed some release.

"Heads up, ladies and gents! Balloons and darts your way! Win a prize! Take a chance! Only one dollar!"

The announcer must have noticed us because he immediately began to beckon Ray and I to come closer.

"Hey there, mister! Wanna win a prize for this lovely lady next to ya? Only a dollar?"

Ray turned to me, wondering if I was interested.

"What do you think? Give it a try, and you can get your pick out of any of the animals?"

"Hmm, sure, but it goes with me."

"Deal!"

A quick shaking of the hands, money exchange, and then it was off to the darts. Ray was surprisingly not the worst player. I mean, the man wields his gun well and shoots better than me at the gun range. Ray paid for ten balloons, and he threw nine out of ten. The announcer's mouth drop resembled a dead fish.

"Wow! Check you out, mister! Wanna go another round?"

Ray turned around, facing me with the puppy dog eyes, hoping I would agree.

"It's up to you, man, but I get the biggest prize."

"Deal."

A shaking of the hands, another brief money exchange, and it was back to the darts. This time, Ray won ten out of ten. The announcer's jaw fell flat to the floor.

"I swear, Ray, it's like you got magic hands!"

He casually shrugged his shoulders and wiped imaginary dust off his shoulders.

"Wow, mister! You've got the magic touch! Want another round?"

"No, thanks. This is it."

"No problem! No problem! You played twice, so pick your prize! The prize that's two times big in size!"

Ray motioned for me to take my choice amidst the colorful, smiley horses, giraffes, cats, dogs, and surprisingly a huge panda.

"Uh, the panda's a beauty. Can I get that one?"

"Sure thing, Ms. Lady."

The announcer quickly hoisted the panda up and out into my arms.

"Thank you."

A wide smile from the announcer gave me goosebumps.

"You like pandas, don't you?"

A nudge from Ray startled me as I buried my face in the stuffed panda's soft fur. It was so sweet and smelled like strawberries.

"Uh, not really, but Jackson always loved them. Whenever we went to the zoo, he would always ask to see pandas."

Ray placed his hand on my shoulder and softly rubbed it.

"Having fun?"

"Yeah. Actually, I—uh—am. I really am. This was such a good idea. Thanks for taking me here, Ray."

"Hey, of course. I told you the carnival helps bring a smile to your face. It's much more relieving than you would think. Now, what's this little guy's name?"

Without hesitation, I answered, "Simba."

Ray's eyebrows furrowed at that.

"Why, Simba?"

"We were supposed to go to Broadway and see the play. He loved the message behind rising above the humiliation and rejection of others. We didn't end up going because he got the flu, and the tickets were too expensive to purchase again. He said I was like Simba because I kicked butt to the worst life had to offer," I said.

Ray hugged me tight, squeezing Simba closer to my chest.

"He was right, you know. You are a lot stronger than you think, Sasha. That's why you were better than Simba. You're amazing. You have a fire that no one can diminish. You need to know that, woman."

A soft chuckle at his words, I absentmindedly raised my hand to his face and smiled as he held my hand.

"Thank you, Ray."

"For what, Sash?"

"For helping me smash a few moles."

We smiled at each other. My cheeks burned the more I squeezed my panda.

"I could just hold you forever, Simba."

PART 5

CHAPTER 30

THE ROMANTIC OBSTACLE

——

"Mmm! So soft and cuddly."

This wasn't like me at all. Could someone tell me why I was obsessing over a damn stuffed panda? Especially one I named Simba? I was relaxing on my couch in my living room after having such a fun time with Ray, who drove me back. Staring at the panda's stitched-on happy face, I couldn't help but kiss its nose.

"Aw, you are adorable. I can't help but love you."

"*Knock! Knock!*"

I reluctantly released Simba to go answer the door.

"Who is it?"

"It's Nay and Max. We need to talk."

My stomach dropped. I didn't want to see them. I had a feeling they would ruin my happy bubble. I couldn't explain why considering they were my partners in crime. I had a feeling Nay would burst my bubble for some reason. I felt like there was something more she wanted to gain aside from justice. I just didn't know what it was. Nay was a firecracker, so I knew I had to get to the bottom of it.

"About what?" I folded my arms and instantly felt my happy bubble pop.

"Can you let us in? So, we can chat, please?"

"Why now? Can't you come back another time?"

"Sasha, please. We have to talk. We're friends, and we need to be open. Just hear me, just ten minutes, just hear me out. Okay?"

"Just ten minutes?"

"Yes, I promise."

Against my better judgment, I decided to hear her out. If she wouldn't play nice, she was outta here.

"Hmm ... fine."

I unfolded my arms and opened the door. Naomi and Max immediately allowed themselves in my living room. I noticed Nay pursed her lips and squinted her eyes quite a bit the longer she saw my panda.

"Sasha?"

"Yes, Nay?"

"Hmm. What's that?" Naomi said in disgust as she pointed at Simba.

"It's a panda, Nay. Isn't it obvious?"

I sat back down on my couch and moved my finger up to point at my forehead, motioning for her to use her brain.

"Uh yeah," she said. "But why is it here?"

"I went out with Ray to a traveling carnival, and he won it for me."

I could immediately sense Nay's disapproval and Max's disappointment. I walked back to my loveseat couch and sat on it.

"I see. It's Ray again. Ray. Ray, Ray, Ray, Ray, oh we love Ray! All we ever hear about is Ray, how Ray is kind, how Ray doesn't believe in revenge, how Ray thinks we are better

than this, yada, yada, yada! Goody, goody, we just *love* Ray!"
Naomi began to make kissy faces.

"Shut up, Nay. But Sasha, seriously. Are you into this guy?"
Max stood in front of me and sat down next to me. He
held my hands and looked straight at me.

"The plan is here. You can't just forget that. Morgan is still
out and about. He needs to get a taste of his own medicine.
I mean, have you been speaking to him lately? Like, when
was the last time you went out with him?"

"I … I haven't been out with him for a while. I've meant
to hit him up, but I've been with Ray. He's honestly such an
amazing person."

"Sasha, I get that, but the plan is still ongoing,"
I squeezed Max's hands back absentmindedly.

"Max, I hear you. I hear what you're saying, both of you.
But for the first time since Jackson and Jane died, I've felt
alive, human. I've been feeling like someone who hasn't been
plagued by anger, hatred, and bullshit this entire time. I finally
feel free! Do you know how long it's been since I've felt like
that? Do you? Do either one of you?" I questioned them.

Naomi scooted over to me and clutched my shoulders.
She stared at me with soft eyes for a few minutes before taking
a deep breath.

"No, I haven't. Not for a long time. Even while fucking
Max and I'm sure for him either."

His jaw dropped at her.

She mouthed a small "O."

"Sorry, Max. But you can still feel like that after the plan
is over."

"Cut to the chase, guys. Why are you even here?"

Naomi looked pointedly at me. "Look, I don't like being
here any more than you like me being here, but—"

"Sasha, we checked his records. He's treating another kid."

At that, my eyes widened bigger than beach balls. I caught her hands off my shoulders.

"What? How do you know that?"

"I stopped by the hospital and spoke to his secretary, I told her I wanted some information for families with sick kids. She got in touch with a support group for me. Surprisingly, I met a few people who have a beef with Morgan."

My throat fell in the dark pit that was my stomach.

"Oh my god, he's never going to stop. Is he?"

Naomi squeezed my hands. "No, Sasha. He won't."

"Every time I'm out with Morgan, it's like I get sucked into this black hole of rage and hatred. I'm angry all the time, and I haven't been sleeping well. I've been lying to Ray for weeks. He's the only good thing I got going for me. I can't hurt him like this, Naomi. I can't lose him too."

I stood and looked down at both of them. Naomi pulled out a photo and stretched her arm out.

"Can you do this for him?"

She pulled another photo. It was an old one of Jackson and his four-teeth smile. I snatched it out of her hand. I had given it to her when we first went over the plan. I couldn't believe she would stoop this low. She pulled another photo out of her pocket.

"Or her? Max's girl?"

She walked over to Simba, picked him up, and threw him on the floor. I immediately scooped him up. I turned angry at her.

"Stop it, Naomi."

She ignored me.

"Or for this creature and what he represents?"

"Stay away from him. This panda and picture are sacred. You have no right, you bitch!"

I went for her throat. Max quickly stood behind me and held my arm back.

"I know it's extreme, but she's trying to show you how important it is for you not to neglect our plan. He won't stop if we don't. You need to stop neglecting Morgan and hit him up. Ask him out for a date this week."

Max lifted my chin with his hand.

"Please remember you can be happy, but the plan can't be forgotten about, Sash. You need to do this."

I nodded my head, set the photo down on the coffee table, held Simba in one arm, and pulled out my phone.

Smacking my lips together, "I need some time to think right now. I'm not ready to just jump back into the plan after feeling so free. Let me consider it. When I'm ready, I'll call Morgan and ask him out."

"Okay, then. We'll give you that. But our ten minutes are up. As promised, we'll leave you alone for the night."

Naomi and Max headed out for the door. Once they were gone, after giving myself an inner pep talk, I decided to dial Morgan's number. I quickly hung up. I took a deep breath.

"Come on, Sasha, you can do this."

I dialed his number again.

La! La! La!

"Hello?"

"Hi Jonathan, it's me, Sasha."

"Sasha! I haven't heard from you. I was wondering if we would speak sometime soon again."

"Yeah, I know, I'm sorry. I've just been really busy, but I was wondering if you wanted to have a picnic near the harbor, maybe sometime this week?"

Both Naomi's and Max's heads were nodding in approval. I rolled my eyes at them.

"Oh yes! I'd love to. I'll check back with you for more info later. I just need to get back to work. I have a few more patients to see tonight."

I clutched my iPhone close and threw my hand in a fist while grimacing at the thought of anyone else under his care.

"Oh sure, let's chat soon. See ya."

"Talk to you soon, Sasha."

Beep! Beep! Beep!

"You did good, Sasha. But remember what you have to do next. It won't be easy."

I rubbed my shoulders. I looked down at Simba in my arms and felt my heart get cut out of my chest.

CHAPTER 31

A RECONFIGURATION OF THE HEART

———

My stomach began doing flips repeatedly. My head felt like it was up in flames, like I was being burned alive. As I clutched my belly, I felt myself losing my breakfast ... again. Thankfully my office had spacious bathrooms.

Ay! Why do I feel like this?

I couldn't help but feel like I needed to end Morgan once and for all, to break free of him because what Naomi said was true, right? Ray is just a distraction. It wasn't a big deal, right? But first, I needed to end things with Ray once and for all. It's for the best. He's just a distraction. Then why did I feel so shitty? I felt the pit of my stomach drop as bile suddenly released from my mouth. Upon finishing, I returned to my desk and flung my arm over my eyes. A small jingle entered my ears as I noticed the caller ID. I popped in a spearmint gum from my purse, hoping it would freshen my breath.

"Hey! Hey! Hey!"

I turned FaceTime to see it was Ray greeting me. Oh great, just what I need. I mentally groaned at whatever he could say.

"Hey, Sasha!"

"Hi, Ray. What's up?"

"I know you're busy, and we have to work soon. I was wondering if you wanted to go see a movie this weekend and maybe grab some dinner at—"

"I can't."

"Wait, I'm sorry, what?"

"I can't, Ray."

He must have sensed anxiety in my voice because Ray's tone turned nervous. He squinted his eyes at me.

"What's going on?"

My stomach knots tightened at hearing his concern.

"No, well yes, just I can't do this anymore."

"What do you mean? Sash? You're scaring me."

"There's nothing wrong. I'm just—I'm just trying to get some stuff intact. I just need to refocus and prioritize some stuff."

"What's going on?"

"Just what I said before, need to prioritize some stuff around. I can't hang out with you as much anymore. Listen, something's come up, and I won't be in town for the next few days. Will you watch the office for me?"

"What? Where are you going?"

"I can't discuss this, Ray. I just need to take some time to myself."

"I see. I suppose there's nothing I can do or say to change your mind."

"You're right. There isn't."

"I see. Well, I'm almost at the office. We can talk about this more in person."

I scoffed at him.

"There's nothing to discuss. We can chat about whatever it is you wish later. We're done, Ray. End of discussion."

Before I could give him any time to respond, I walked into my office. Ray followed me a few feet away.

"Ay"

I rubbed my temples and stomach, knowing of the hell hole soon to come. I lay my face in my hands, utterly terrified.

Ding!

The door signaled Ray was here, and I immediately rose my head.

"Okay, Sasha. What's going on? This isn't like you. Let's talk. We are discussing what the hell you said to me over the phone."

Ray folded his arms and stood in front of me.

"What the hell is going on, Sasha?"

"Nothing, Ray. I just need to refocus and reprioritize."

Ray slammed my desk and made me jump.

"Oh, don't give me that crap, Sasha! Something is going on, and you are going to tell me!"

I quickly stood up face to face to Ray.

"Don't you talk to me like that! If I want to change my life around, I can do that without needing your goddamn permission!"

"No, you do! That's where you're wrong. I'm here to help you! To guide you! To show you life is beautiful and doesn't need to be full of grudges, revenge, or hatred!"

"Oh yes, it is! Life is shit, and while you can have blissful moments, revenge and hatred are much stronger, Ray!"

His eyes widened, and he took a step back.

In a quiet voice, he asked, "What do you mean by that?"

Oh shit. My stomach fell into my butt. I realized I'd just fucked up.

"Nothing."

Ray's squinted eyes pierced through my soul. He walked closer until I could almost hear his heartbeat.

"Are you saying what I think you're saying? You're still trying to get revenge on Morgan, aren't you?"

My prolonged silence must have lit up a light bulb in Ray's mind.

"I can't believe this!" He scoffed at me. "After everything, you've just lied?"

"Ray, you don't understand. I ..."

"No, I understand perfectly. You were pretending to have a friendship with me while plotting a sick murder behind it all."

"Not a murder but a—"

"Sasha! I don't give a fuck what it actually was! All I know is—you know what? It doesn't matter anymore because I'm done. I'm done."

Ray walked back to his desk and began gathering everything on it inside of his bag. It puzzled me.

"What? What? What are you doing?"

Without even looking back at me, he responded, "I'm packing up my stuff. I can't work here anymore."

"Why not?" Ray looked pissed.

"Seriously? You lied to me and aren't going to put out this fire of revenge. You just want to add lighter fluid and burn your life down to shit. Goodbye, Sasha." He grabbed his bag and headed out the door.

I walked up to him. "Ray, you have no idea how much you have meant to me. I have truly valued your friendship these last few years. I could never open to anyone after Jane like you and after my shitty traumas. You were a light at the end of the tunnel. You have no idea how long I've been suffering. With you, I've finally found relief."

***

"Sasha, get in here, you piece of …!" My newest foster dad yelled after me as I ran downstairs from his horrifying and dark home to the safety of my car.

"You won't make it on your own, Sasha! You are worthless!"

***

"Mommy! Mommy! Don't leave me alone!" I was holding on to my drug-addicted mother's hand as tightly as I could, fighting against a suit-clad woman. But my mother loosened her grip from me and let go of my hand.

"Sorry, Sasha. But I can't be a mother in my condition. You'll be fine without me. Besides, the resemblance you bear toward your father in both your appearance and personality already tells me what type of life you'll live. I can't be around you anymore."

"Mommy, no!" The lady began dragging me away before eventually realizing I would no longer resist the more tears dripped on my face.

***

"I'm sorry, Sasha, but I can't do this anymore. I love you, but we lost our son. How can we move on from this?" Jane began pacing around our living room. I grabbed her hands and lifted a strand of hair from her face.

"Jane, I promise you, as long as we're together, we'll be okay." Jane removed her hands and walked away from me.

"You can't promise that, Sasha! You, you just can't!

***

"Ray, pain and suffering have been the only things that have accompanied me throughout the years."

"I care about you, Sasha, deeply. I just hope you can soon remember that anger, revenge, or hatred aren't important.

You'll lose out on the most important things if you don't forget about Morgan. Goodbye, Sasha."

His words were sharp as a peeled onion that I began to shed tears. In the midst of my crying, I noticed a small, shiny object on Ray's desk—a tiny brooch in the shape of a rose. I clutched it in a fist and held it close to my heart. He turned around to me with hurt eyes.

"At least we had a chance to find that damn bird. Lord knows how tedious Lucio was to find. I'll miss you, Sasha."

"Oh God, I'm sorry, Ray. But I have to. I have to." I began to cry, but I knew my next task.

I picked up the phone and began dialing Morgan.

CHAPTER 32

SASHA FINALLY SUCCEEDS

___

"This was such a good idea, Sasha. We were at a picnic in the park with apple cider, turkey wraps, baked chips, and a long blanket. It's all perfect."

With Ray out of the way, I was free to focus on Morgan. I called him up at the end of the day and planned to spend Saturday together in a remote spot in the park.

The park was relatively new. We had a big tree shading us from the hot sun with a nice view of a small river to greet us. For some reason, staring at the river reminded me no matter what happens in this life or the next, the waves will continue moving back and forth.

"I'm glad you're enjoying it, Jonathan. I am too."

We continued eating our lunch in peace or as much peace as I could try to give myself. He was a perfect gentleman, and it reminded me of Ray. It began to make me sick.

"Sasha, I've been having a good time with you. I'd love to see you more often. I hope it's okay if I ask you to consider becoming my girlfriend."

Since I was still chewing my sandwich, I nearly choked while fighting back the urge to gag.

"Oh! Um, sure, Jonathan. Yes, I would love to."

Morgan had a small smile at my response.

"I'm glad, Sasha."

I stared at him straight in the eyes and leaned in closer. I looked deep into his brown eyes with a faux lust and desire. Watching his cheeks turn into the same color as the roses surrounding us, perfecting the moment of entrapment. I winked at him, sealing my ambush into place.

"Yes."

Morgan's face had the same charming, winning smile he always had whenever he got something he wanted.

"Therefore, Sasha as my new girlfriend, would you like to have dinner at my place tomorrow night?"

"Why not tonight? The longer we must wait, the more anxious I get to want to spend some more time with you sooner."

Morgan grinned at me and gave me a gentle kiss on the lips.

"Okay, okay, Sasha. Let's have dinner tonight at my place and maybe movies after?"

I gave him a small peck.

"Sounds good because I have a feeling everything will be amazing after tonight. I have a feeling tonight will be the start of a new beginning for you and me."

It wasn't a lie. Taking a sip of cider, I passionately kissed my *boyfriend.*

"I have a feeling the longer you spend time with me, Jonathan, the more you will like me. Don't you think so?"

Morgan laughed and shook his head at me.

"I hope so, Sasha, because I may have some surprises for you too."

For some reason, that statement unsettled me, but I knew I needed to win the war if he won this battle.

"Can I ask what you have planned for tonight then, Jonathan? How do you plan on surprising your new girlfriend? I mean I have to tell you, I don't come cheap. I appreciate being wined and dined."

Morgan leaned in a little too close for comfort. I could smell his cologne.

He smiled widely at me. "I'm old-fashioned in that I believe a lady deserves romance to the fullest. But you know, ladies can always amaze a gentleman too," Morgan smirked at me.

"Oh, trust me, doc. You've seen nothing like me yet."

All I needed to do next was text Max and Naomi about tonight, and this charade would soon be over.

CHAPTER 33

THE FINALE: WHEN HEAVEN FINALLY MEETS HELL

PART 1

"Sasha, I hope you enjoy tonight's meal. I made you some salmon with brown rice and feta cheese salad. I also had some white wine as well for you to enjoy."

Morgan poured me a light cup of wine before sitting down across from me at a small table outside in his backyard. Unsurprisingly, he had a relatively large mansion surrounded by a neighborhood full of houses you would see on *Food Network*. The candles and lights surrounding us were enormous and provided a disgusting romantic setting. Like my "boyfriend" wanted to surprise his "girlfriend" for a "special time tonight."

After the picnic, Morgan and I made plans to meet up for dinner at his home before going our separate ways so we could get dressed up and ready for the night.

"It's delicious, John. Thanks, honey," I said as I saw Morgan's winking face.

"I appreciate it, my love. You know I live to please you. Now, let's not sit here with our tummies rumbling. Let's dig in."

Morgan clapped his hands together and settled in to feast. Our homemade dinner in his small mansion wasn't too bad. I had an inkling Morgan, my "boyfriend," would want something more tonight. Thankfully, we both managed to enjoy the food and hardly felt the need to talk. Giving me an emphasis on my plan, it would be over and finally end tonight.

"Thanks for dinner tonight, honey. It was good. Do you mind if I asked you for another glass of wine?"

"Of course not, my darling, here."

Morgan poured me another glass of wine, and we continued drinking. I saw a few goldfish in his nearby pond swim by the garden. As I sipped my wine, I decided to turn things up a notch. I knew it would be perfect tonight.

"Honey?"

"Yes, Sash?"

"Would I be too forward if I asked if I could stay a while longer tonight?"

Morgan grinned at my question.

"Why, certainly, Sasha. It's chilly in here anyway. We could go inside and get some coffee and throw a movie on. I can drive you home afterward if that's fine?"

"Yes, why not? That's a good idea."

We went inside and sat down on his shiny white couch, sipping wine and sharing a blanket he had near the table. Morgan turned on the TV, and we channel surfed until we settled on a slasher nineties horror film. About ten minutes passed before I felt Morgan snuggle closer to me and place his head on my shoulder. Resisting the urge to roll my eyes, I stretched my arm out and cuddled him close. He placed a kiss on my forehead. I chose to up my game a notch. I slid my hand down and gave his leg a gentle squeeze. Morgan turned his head and looked at me, leaned in, and gave me a gentle kiss on my lips. I pushed him back and smiled softly at him.

"Honey, do you mind grabbing us some more wine? I have a feeling it's going to be a good night."

"Sure, darling."

Morgan slid off the couch in search of wine. As soon as he was gone, I took a small packet from my pocket. It contained crushed-up sleeping pills. I slipped them into his glass of wine that, thankfully, he left on the coffee table. Gently shaking the glass to dissolve the pills, I waited for Morgan's return.

"Sasha! I have two bottles, just in case. Red or white?"

"White, please."

"Perfect! Same as me as I didn't finish my earlier glass."

Morgan poured us more wine. Soon after, we cuddled close under the blanket and began to kiss again. Morgan pulled away and looked me square in the eyes.

"I like you, Sasha. I really do."

My eyes widened at him. He's good. But I had to continue with the charade for only so long.

"Ditto, Jonathan."

He smiled at that.

"But let's drink some more wine. Hmm?"

Morgan took a few more sips of wine before cuddling and kissing more. The more we kissed, I felt Morgan slowly succumb to slumber. As he began to kiss my neck, I sensed him getting sleepier and sleepier until finally falling flat to dreamland. I flicked his neck to check his unconscious state. Once verified, I knew it was time to get to work.

"Sweet dreams, doctor dearest." I lightly flicked his head, silently relishing in his unconscious state.

CHAPTER 34

THE FINALE: WHEN HEAVEN FINALLY MEETS HELL

PART 2

───

After roughly dragging Morgan down the stairs to his basement, thanks to his heavy weight, it took a minute even to begin moving him. I had finally grabbed a chair from his living room and used it to get him into the basement. He didn't have stairs, thank goodness, but his basement was located behind a door a few feet away from his neat and modern-day style kitchen. Regardless, I quickly bounded him by some rope, put duct tape on his mouth items all from my home, and once I realized it was time, I splashed water on his face. When he didn't respond, I slapped him around a few times until he began to stir. I mean, it was around seven to eight pills of melatonin. He didn't need sleep for long.

"Wakey, wakey, sleepyhead."

I ripped the duct tape off his mouth fast and easily. I slapped him again. Morgan slowly shifted and turned his head, moving his head toward me.

"Huh, waa—what's—what's going on?"

"Oh, look who's finally awake. Thank goodness because that means this game is finally over. Thank God for that!"

Morgan's sleepy face contoured into confusion. He was bounded next to a radiator while sitting down in one of his fancy living room chairs. I had to admit his basement was empty and well-kept, aside from a few Christmas and Halloween decorations tossed aside with a terrible shade of gray all around. A medium-sized fake skeleton close to the chair gave off a strange vibe.

I began to pace, hiding a small knife clutched behind my back. I took a deep breath while feeling my heart do somersaults as the moment finally arrived. With every step I took, there was an echo emphasizing my footsteps, beautifully making me appear more sinister to him.

As I walked closer to him, confident and daring, Morgan tried to move away from me.

"Waaa—what—what do you mean?"

"You killed my son. You took his life. I found the proof in your hospital records room. You had lots of files in there, especially where you took the lives of other people's children as well, including Max Sandoval and Naomi de Alba. It seems you have a history of using a whole bunch of ricin, and you inject it in their little systems, and you just get off watching them die."

"Nay—Naomi de Alba? You mean the crazy lady?"

I immediately slapped him.

"She's not crazy! She's the mother of another child you murdered! As am I, as is Max! You took our children away! Now the time has come to get revenge and destroy you!"

I picked up a hammer and swiftly slammed it down on Morgan's knee. He screamed in pain, his face turning red, neck pulsing. Tears rolled down his face, and he whimpered, his leg trembling. I smiled.

"Stop, please! Stop, you crazy bitch!"

I further slammed the hammer into his knee. His cries of pain excited me to cause him more pain.

"Please stop! I beg you!"

I stopped and eased up with the hammer. A fire began to build up inside me.

"Stop! You want me to stop? Isn't that what you should have done to my kid, Nay's, and Max's kids. Stop, had mercy, and actually do your job?"

I continued to use the hammer on Morgan. His screams of pain edged me on until I heard my iPhone buzz. I dropped the hammer on the floor. Max and Naomi were on their way. When I sent them the signal that Morgan was ready, I texted them his door code. They made their way into the soundproof room with no cameras secretly made by me a few moments ago, thanks to random blankets and quilts I found to cover the walls and a small window near the door.

They both arrived staring at him with rage in their eyes and held both my hands. This was it. The spiders caught the fly in their trap, and he couldn't escape now.

Naomi walked right up to Morgan and slapped him hard in the face.

"What's wrong? Don't you remember me? Do you need another reminder?"

I slapped him across the face.

"Do you need another one?"

I slapped him across his cheek.

"Another one?"

I punched him in his Adam's apple.

"How 'bout another?"

This time, when I punched him, I reached his left eye and corners of his nose.

"Remember me now?"

Morgan's face was now bloody. Before Naomi could continue hitting him, Max pulled her away and looked her straight in the eyes.

"Nay! This is not what we are here for. We aren't here to torture, punch, nor kill! We can play around with him for a bit, but we won't be calling the cops anytime soon. If we get caught torturing him, we can get in trouble. So, with enough time, our prints won't be found on him if we wear gloves and are as careful as possible. We'll be gone by the time the police come, and we have enough to put him away."

"No! I wanna kill him."

"No, Nay! We agreed!"

As they continued to bicker, I noticed a familiar vibration coming from my pocket.

"Damn it. It's Ray!"

They both looked at me in surprise. Morgan's eyes were slowly closing and opening again.

"Don't answer it! Who cares?" yelled Naomi.

"I have to! He will know something's wrong!"

"Just text him then!" screamed Max.

"We don't text! We call! It's our agreement! Just keep him quiet, and you two shut up!"

I motioned for them to duct tape Morgan's mouth again. I decided to leave the room and go upstairs for more quietness. I found myself in the kitchen. Once the coast was clear, I slid the iPhone and heard Ray's voice.

"Sasha!"

"Ray, I really can't talk right now. A little busy here."

"I don't give a fuck! You need to give me back my mother's rose brooch. The one I left on my desk before I quit the practice. She wore it all of the time before she died."

"I told you I would return it to you another time."

Morgan groaned as he began to rouse again quite loudly. Who knew when the guy woke up or stretched, he had to be a damn near screamer?

"What the hell was that?"

"Nothing, Ray. I just stretched."

"You don't make that sound when you stretch, especially not that way. What the hell is going on, Sasha? I'm trying to tell you that you need to know what I just found out."

"I don't want to hear it, Ray. You'll get your brooch soon, all right?"

"Sasha! Your friend Naomi isn't who you think she is!"

I was taken aback at that.

"What do you mean? Ray, what the hell are you talking about?"

"I knew that would get you to listen and shut up. But here, Naomi is not—"

A loud screeching sound suddenly arrived.

"Sasha!"

I recognized it as Naomi's voice. I took it as my cue to return.

"What was that, Sasha?"

"Nothing. Everything is fucking fine, Ray. Jesus! By the way, why the fuck do you care? I have no reason to give you any kind of explanation since you left me and our relationship behind."

Tears streamed down my cheeks, and I felt a tap on my shoulder, Nay motioning me to speed it up.

"Anyways, Ray, I gotta go. Bye. You'll get the damn brooch soon.

"Sasha, I did care about you, but you were too …"

"Goodbye, Ray."

"Sasha, wait!"

CHAPTER 35

THE FINALE: WHEN HEAVEN FINALLY MEETS HELL

PART 3

I put the phone away, walked back downstairs to the basement, walked up to the others who, unlike Morgan, were just standing around waiting for my next move. Morgan was bleeding heavily from his head down to his neck. I grabbed the hammer off the floor. Just as I prepared to swing at Morgan with my friend the hammer, Max suddenly grabbed my arm.

"Sasha, no! He's had enough. Any more and you kill him."

I shrugged him off.

"He deserves to suffer, Max."

"No, Sasha. We can call the police. We have the evidence."

"Believe me. It's too late to call the cops. Besides, I need to hear him say it."

"He's dead, so what?"

We all turned to see Morgan fully awake with blood pumping down his face.

"What did you just say?"

"Your kids are dead. Who cares? It's all over. I knew from the moment you bumped into me at the supermarket. Have to say I didn't think you were so naive to go all the way through with this plan of yours to actually agree to date me. Also, before I forget, thanks for saying hello to my nana for me. At least she will always be with me now. She's never disappearing from me again."

Morgan spits out blood after he speaks.

"How? How the hell …"

"Randomly bumping into me, suddenly going out, trying to get me drunk plus as a private detective, I wondered how long it would be until I could get in your pants as your reward for playing the role well. Also, did you really think Amy wouldn't let me know of whoever asks about my past? She adores me."

"So, you knew all along?"

"Well, not exactly, but I figured after that first dinner date we had. When you went to the bathroom and 'accidentally left your phone behind.' I saw your messages, 'Go for it.' 'Seduce him.' 'He deserves to pay.' You were like a chameleon, always changing colors. Just like your wife, Jane," he said.

My heart immediately dropped at his words.

"What do you mean, Jane?" Morgan snickered at me.

"Let's just say Jane wanted to go on a little scavenger hunt just like you, and she ended up getting in my way."

Naomi stepped up and smacked Morgan across the face. He recoiled, blood splattering on the floor, and then he spat and chuckled, looking up at her. She did it again before turning to me.

"I told you to be careful, Sasha! Now, our plan is in ruins," Naomi scolded me.

"How did I not know? How?"

Naomi rolled her eyes at me.

Morgan cleared his throat before straightening up in his seat and looking directly at me, "Also, there's also something you should know about your friend over there, Naomi. She's a liar."

Max and I looked at Nay in confusion.

"Nay, what is he talking about?"

She shook her head and shrugged.

"Ms. Naomi here is lying to you. What did she tell you? That I killed her kid? Ha! She doesn't have any. She never did. She stalked me after a first date years ago because I slammed the door on her. She just wasn't it for me. I wasn't interested in her. She came after me a few times, begging for a chance, but I eventually got a restraining order against her. One night, I was walking a date home, and she followed us, nearly killed the poor bitch by bashing her head on the sidewalk, breaking the rules of that damn restraining order. But that didn't stop her. Every time she got out and claimed to change, she'd be right back to stalking me and whoever I brought to my house. The last time I spoke to little Ms. Naomi, I told her to fuck off. I wanted nothing to do with her, but she said she would find a way to pay because she would make me hers. She's had it in for me ever since. No matter where I moved, what I said, or what I did, there was never truly getting rid of her."

Max squinted his eyes at Naomi.

"Nay, is this true?"

Naomi huffed in annoyance. "So what the fuck if it is true? He's still a bad guy who killed your kids and broke my heart. Let's get back to murdering him, shall we?"

Naomi pulled out a Smith and Wesson M and P Shield from her pocket and pointed it at Morgan, whose eyes widened at the sight of it.

I immediately blocked her aim.

"Wait, you mean this whole time you lied? What about the file about your kid I found in the hospital records room?"

Naomi lowered her gun but still stood in front of me.

"I made it up. I scanned some fake documents and figured you would want revenge for Jackson. Since you and I met Max in the hospital, I figured we could make a great team. You would be surprised how easy it is to fake docs. No wonder why kids make up fake IDs."

I shook my head, caught a glimpse of a baffled Max through the corner of my eye, and swallowed hard before turning over to Naomi.

"What about the girl I saw you visit outside the hospital room?"

"Real cancer patient but not my real kid. I just popped in and out of her room."

Max stood in front of me, blocking me from Naomi.

"So, you took advantage of my pain, our pain? Our grief? All because of this asshole rejecting your ass? What the fuck is wrong with you?"

"A lot of things, but that's beside the point. Now move!"

Naomi shoved Max, who immediately stood his ground and pushed her back. Morgan began screaming, trying to get away from them. He was unsuccessful, considering he was still bound to the chair with duct tape. His arms and hands turned red and appeared immensely sweaty. He did succeed in toppling over in the chair, however. A nearby gun cocked. A very familiar voice popped in.

"Freeze! Drop the weapon! Put your hands up!"

Ray held his Gen 4 Glock 19 in his hands and motioned for Max and Naomi to separate. She raised her hands above her head while still holding her gun. She slowly backed away from Max. She no longer aimed at Morgan. Once they did, Ray stood a few feet away. He still held his gun, ready to shoot if necessary.

"I knew you were going to do something stupid, Sasha, but I didn't think this stupid."

Ray put the gun back in his holster and gave me a pissed-off face. Ray took a quick survey around the room before looking back at me.

"You lied to me. You told me you were done with this. That you realized Jackson wouldn't want this, and you lied. You lied to my face."

Ray's voice sounded so hurt and accusatory that I couldn't deny him. I did lie.

"How the hell did you get in here, Ray?" I yelled.

"Sasha, I'm a detective. I got access to finding security codes, breaking locks, making copies of keys, and this creep, or maybe you three just forgot to lock the door! Not exactly a genius idea, woman!"

I rolled my eyes and looked back at Naomi and Max, who shrugged.

"Don't look at us, Sash!"

"I can't believe you decided to disregard everything I told you and just went for this, Sasha," Ray's voice lowered slightly.

"Ray, you aren't a parent. You don't know how it felt to have had your dreams of a family crushed. He took it all. I need to make sure he pays for it. I'm sorry I lied, but I had to ensure this wouldn't go to shit."

Ray shook his head at me.

"I may have been angry. I still am, but I made you a promise once before. I am still here for you, Sasha. I'm not going to let you destroy yourself."

"Hey!" Naomi yelled.

Ray and I peered over at Max and Naomi.

"That's so sweet. I hate sweet! This would have all gone smoothly if you hadn't interfered."

Ray walked closer to Max and Naomi.

"Unlike the two of you, I was being a friend. Considering her feelings, asking her how she was feeling, checking up on her, singing her lullabies, holding her while she cried over her loss, and just being there whenever she needed me. A few things you call 'interfering,' but actually, it means I was being a friend."

Max got pissed at that and walked into Ray's face.

"Unlike you, 'being a friend,' I was there to hear her frustrations on this plan, hear her anger between her and all of this bullshit, and just being a source for her to vent. So, don't you dare come here pretending like you are friend of the year, bitch okay?"

Ray got even closer to Max.

"Call me that again."

"Bitch."

"That's it."

I stood in between them.

"Stop it now! Don't be stupid."

Ray and Max glared sharply at each other but maintained a good distance away. Naomi now aimed her gun at Morgan, whose eyes widened in fear.

Naomi and I watched and hollered at them to stop. When they didn't, Naomi sent over a solution of her own. Naomi's gun went off ... the room grew silent. Time stood frozen as we, including Morgan, saw Naomi shoot her gun toward the ceiling. Only once she noticed the men had stopped fighting, she then lowered her gun.

"Now that I have your attention. Let's get back to business. You know my intentions, Sash. We know yours, Max, and

Ray. Which you aren't innocent, but I plan to get this over with once and for all."

She walked closer and pointed her gun at Morgan, who squirmed in his seat. Ray and Max raced to her. I stood in my place. "No!" She aimed at them. "Don't you come any closer. I'm warning you."

I slowly walked over to her and immediately tackled her.

"Sasha, stop it! Let go!"

Naomi and I began fighting over the gun.

Ray shouted at us to stop, "Drop it *now!*" We didn't listen to him, and Naomi nearly shot my foot.

Ray aimed his gun at Naomi. My stomach dropped at the sight.

"I've got one too. I can do this all night."

Naomi rolled her eyes and took another step. "Shut the fuck up."

"I'm serious, Naomi. Don't screw up any further. This can all end here."

I could swear Nay shed a tear.

"No, it can't. No one rejects me nor tells me what to do. I will never stop until he's dead and buried."

Naomi pulled her gun at Morgan. My heart dropped to the pit of my stomach.

"Nay, no!"

"Noooooooooo!" Max jumped in to stop her.

Naomi's gun went off first, blowing half Morgan's head away, and the next moment a bullet pushed her into the wall as Ray discharged his own weapon. Morgan slumped over completely while handcuffed to his basement chair slumped to the floor. Naomi slowly slid the wall until she hit the floor and slightly tilted her head. Blood began to drip down both of their bodies, mixing together to create a dark crimson red.

Ray lowered his glock. Max fell to the floor, groaning and moaning in pain, clutching his bloody leg.

"Oh, what the fuck? The bitch shot me!"

I ran to Max's side.

"Max, are you okay?"

He looked at me like I was an idiot.

"Do I look okay?"

"I … I can't believe I did this, but I warned her."

Ray's eyes began watering. Silent tears flowed down his entire face. Ray's crying face struck a chord with me.

"I warned her. If she was going to do this …"

Max's wide eyes paralyzed me with the shock flowing down my veins. It felt like ice-cold water sliding down my back.

"You … you killed her."

Wiping his tears away, Ray placed his gun back in his holster before looking back at me.

"She wanted to kill him, and she did."

"Now, we can all agree to put this behind us while I call the police. We collaborate, get our stories straight and do what we have to do to go home tonight."

Ray looked at the both of us, anticipating an answer. He put his hand out in between us.

"Agreed?" Max placed his hand on top of Ray's.

"Agreed. Sasha?"

The two stared at me. My entire body was ice cold while my chest felt volcano hot. But I knew Ray would help me. So, I did the right thing and placed my hand on top of both of theirs.

"Agreed, and you two were right. I didn't need to torture nor kill him. I'm not the villain, but I'm no hero. I'm making my own destiny with my inner darkness."

CHAPTER 36

THE TRIAL RESOLUTION OF SASHA

———

Ray and I were back at the Sunset Diner. It had been such a rough night. Neither one of us got any sleep. Max received his discharge from the hospital, and he decided to go to his daughter's grave. He said he needed a moment alone to think and just relax. We understood and promised to call him within a few days.

We called the police but collaborated our stories before they came. It looked like after killing Morgan, Naomi turned the gun on herself before we could stop her. No evidence proved otherwise. A blond-haired waitress appeared before us with rosy cheeks and a white uniform with a red apron.

"Hi there, can I get you anything?" I shook my head no. My stomach turned to knots thinking of any kind of breakfast.

"No, thank you, just water and a black coffee. Thanks," Ray said with a fake small smile on his face.

"Same for me, I'm not hungry, thank you. Just water with ice."

The waitress nodded before leaving our booth. She quickly returned with two ice-cold glasses of water with small ice cubes and a small cup of black coffee for Ray.

"Just the thought of food makes me want to vomit, honestly." Ray nodded at me in agreement before taking a sip of water.

"I hear you. This whole thing has been on my mind. I can't touch a thing. But I can touch this."

Ray immediately pulled out a small flask out of his pocket and began pouring it into his coffee. He then picked up a small spoon and began mixing the contents. Upon completion, he then took a long sip.

"Mmh, tequila hits the spot." He offered it to me, but I shook my head.

"No thanks, I think I'm good. Just water, and you should lay off that crap too."

Ray placed his glass down and looked at me. I decided to cut the tension with a butter knife.

Closing my eyes, I can still recall Naomi's bloody form and Morgan getting zipped up in a black garbage bag—or at least one that looked like it belonged in the dumpster—and lifted inside an ambulance. Flashes of red, blue, and orange swirled around us, and the blasting volume of sirens began to unsettle me so much.

A man came up to me, Max, and Ray standing together outside Morgan's house. He wore a heavy beige-colored over-coat, his skin was slightly olive-colored, and he pulled out a badge in front of us, it said "Sanchez."

"Hello there, my name is Detective Michael Sanchez from the homicide unit here down in the Carolinas. I understand you three have been under a lot of stress and trauma tonight. Can you tell me what you remember?"

My stomach dropped at that. A small squeeze from Ray slightly comforted me.

"Yeah, I can explain, Detective Sanchez. Unfortunately, it was a murder-suicide. Naomi shot Dr. Jonathan Morgan in cold blood, it appears she's been stalking him for years, and he had been running away from her. It seems like she had found him and shot him to death. Upon realizing what she'd done, she killed herself. We heard the shots, and when we found her, she was barely breathing. Before we could call 9-1-1, she had admitted everything."

Detective Sanchez listened intently and took notes. He nodded while Ray recanted the agreed lie.

"Uh-huh. I see. Thank you. Did she say anything else?"

Ray shook his head.

"Just the confession. She passed before we could ask anything else."

Sanchez nodded again.

"Okay, well, thank you for your time. I'll be in touch. You all are free to go now."

Sanchez politely lowered his head and walked away. Ray, Max, and I all looked at each other and softly nodded at one another.

Whispering, "Let's get out of here. I need to go home and just sleep."

"Let's head out, guys. We didn't do anything wrong. Let's go," said Ray.

We all walked to Ray's car.

"So, are we going to talk about the elephant in the room or what?" Ray looked at me in confusion.

"What do you mean?"

"You know what I mean, the fact you came looking to tell me the information you found about Naomi and the fact you killed her just like that!" I lowered my voice at that.

"Shut up, Sasha! I did what I had to do, and you know that. Plus, we agreed not to talk about it ever again, remember?" Ray looked around us, making sure the public wouldn't hear us.

"I know, but it's just that—" Ray raised a finger to his lips, motioning for me to be quiet.

"Zip it, woman!"

"I—"

"Zip"!"

"It—"

"Zip!"

"Just—"

"Zip it!"

A few customers began to look around us. I raised my hands in surrender.

"Okay, you win. I'm done." I sighed deeply.

"Thank you," Ray leaned back in his seat.

"I just— thanks, Ray."

He looked up at me.

"For what?"

"For saving me ... from myself even when I didn't realize the spiral I was placing myself in, and thanks for saving my life. I don't know how far I would have taken it. I'm not a killer, but I was blinded by rage."

"I get it."

I raised my eyebrows at him in surprise.

"No, I mean I get it, Sasha. He took what you and Max wanted most, a family. Naomi took advantage of you too by bullying you two and pretending to be someone she wasn't. What I don't get is why you didn't just go to the cops and move on from your hatred?"

"To be honest, I couldn't tell you why either. Jackson getting sick, and Jane ... I thought she left, but Morgan took her from me too. I wanted a chance to unleash it all at once. I guess Morgan was the perfect target."

Ray reached out over to me across the table and gently squeezed my hand. He smiled at me.

"At least, it's all over now, and you can start fresh."

"See, that's the thing. I wouldn't know where to begin," I told Ray.

I looked up at our joined hands again and directly into Ray's eyes.

"Perhaps, you could consider coming back to the office and working at the practice again with me?" I asked Ray, hoping he would. He laughed at me.

"Well, I'm not sure, but we'll just have to wait and see. Anything could change us for the better, Sasha."

Ray winked at me. I giggled and grinned at him.

"Oh, yes, things definitely will, Ray."

ACKNOWLEDGMENTS

—

Hey there, ClueFinders!

First and foremost, I'd like to thank my family and loved ones. Mom, dad, Johanna, Michael—a big thank you. You were amazing for always encouraging me to write the book and helping me make this lifelong dream a reality! Thanks, Mom and Dad, for constantly reminding me to eat whenever I had late writing nights and could even barely remember to sleep! Thanks, Dad, for the best homemade oat milk iced coffees that tasted better than Starbucks! No shade to them, but they were free! Thanks, Johanna, for always telling me this little idea would eventually become something extraordinary and always having faith in me growing up! Thank you, Grandma and Grandpa, for always hearing me read and write in front of you even when you couldn't understand it because it was all in English and I could barely write in Spanish!

Thank you so much to my beta readers, Melissa, Yenick, Davidia, and Francis. You all provided such helpful feedback and thoughtful critiques that eventually made this book create more suspense along the way! A special thank you to Melissa and Yenick for consistently sending in your edits and even helping me make sense of what I was trying to say sometimes.

Thank you to everyone who preordered my book on the campaign site, Indiegogo. I can't even describe how much emotional, mental, and especially financial stress was lifted off my shoulders with each of your purchases! Thank you for also giving me the hope that people out there believed in my dream and in this book. Thank you, Eric Koester, Carol Yee, Francis Merencillo, Professor Russell Eliot Dale, Jeremy Abarno, Nia Rainer, Danielle Rizzitelli, Coco Shin, Yasania Barrilla, Samiha Makawi, Johanna Briones, Melissa Tejada, Carlos Alonso, Geronimo Branagan, Kadija Doumbia, Rahin Ahmed, Yenick Gonzalez, Deanna Garcia, Perla Tolentino, Laura Macaddino, Andre Smith, Grace Romero, Hadja Fatoumata Doumbouya, Arvyn Gutierrez, Ivan Miranda, Keyona Davis, Ilia Epifanov, Andrew Clarke, Sara Miranda, Miguel Barrilla Sr, Davidia Boykins, Joel Urena, Natalie Nunez, Miguel Barrilla Jr, Danielle Rizzitelli, Arcania Jaquez, Sarai Bosques, Lissette Cedeno, Melissa Gordon-Ring, Kelly Larrea, Sully Torres, Blanca Chalen, Jesus Lara, Isaiah Reyes, Shannon Wilson, Matthew Shields, Ivonne Alicia Romero Romero, for believing in this dream since the beginning!

Thank you to my college and high school friends and professors, who I can call mis amigos especially Professor Gabrielle Kappes, Zarin, and Marissa, for just being there and an awesome group of smiles!

Lastly, a HUGE THANK YOU to New Degree Press, especially Eric Koester, Sandy Huffman, Ilia Epifanov, Brian Bies, Haley Newlin, and fellow author colleague Nia Rainer for first mentioning this program to me and affirming that writing, publishing, and becoming an author are not too difficult to achieve! Thank you to everyone single one of you for helping ensure for a middle-class, Ecuadorian Italian-Spanish speaking daughter of immigrants in NYC who always dreamed of being an author become a beautiful reality!